B I O E T H I C S

Dilemmas in Modern Medicine

Ann E. Weiss

ENSLOW PUBLISHERS, INC.

Bloy St. & Ramsey Ave.   P.O. Box 38
Box 777   Aldershot
Hillside, N.J. 07205   Hants GU12 6BP
U.S.A.   U.K.

Library of Congress Cataloging in Publication Data

Weiss, Ann E., 1943-
  Bioethics: dilemmas in modern medicine.

  Bibliography: p.
  Includes index.
  Summary: Examines the moral aspects of health care and biological experiments, including such issues as abortion, the rights of patients, mercy killing, and genetic engineering.
  1. Medical ethics. 2. Bioethics. [1. Medical ethics. 2. Bioethics] I. Title.
R724.W36   1985   174'.2   85-11608
ISBN 0-89490-113-3

Printed in the United States of America

10 9 8 7 6 5 4

This book is dedicated to
my friend Margot
with love

ACKNOWLEDGMENT

The author thanks Daniel Callahan, director of the Hastings Center, for reviewing the manuscript and for the valuable suggestions he offered.

Contents

1

Introducing Bioethics

Mary, age twenty-seven, is three months pregnant and very happy about it. Now, though, she's ill—sore throat, temperature, rash, a feeling of tiredness. Worried, Mary goes to her doctor, and he confirms her fears. She has German measles.

German measles is a mild disease—except when the victim is a pregnant woman. Then it can be devastating. Fetuses exposed to the German measles virus during the first three months of their development have a 90 percent chance of being born handicapped. Their disabilities are likely to include blindness, deafness, damage to the internal organs, and mental retardation. In 20 percent of fetuses affected by the virus, these handicaps will be very severe indeed.

Mary dreads the prospect of giving birth to a handicapped child. Yet the alternative is abortion. Many people, including Mary's own husband, believe that abortion amounts to murder. Still, Mary wonders: Is it right to bear a child whom she knows ahead of time will suffer, as hers is likely to do?

Billy is a three-year-old boy with blond hair, blue eyes—and a serious liver disease. Doctors have told the boy's parents that he must have a healthy new liver. Without it, he will die within a few weeks. A liver transplant operation is possible for Billy, the doctor informs the parents, but it will cost a lot of money— over $150,000. And the hospital where the operation would be performed insists on payment *before* admitting Billy.

For Billy's parents, payment is impossible. His father has been out of work for months. There are three other children to care for. No insurance company or public welfare program will agree to pay the bill. Must Billy die, just because his family is not rich?

Susan and David are newlyweds. They want children, but they are fearful. Each comes from a family with a history of producing children who are born with the same rare fatal disease. Any children they have will run an extremely high risk of also having that disease.

Is there any way David and Susan can be sure of having healthy children? In the future, there may be. Already, scientists are finding ways to alter the structure of genes. Genes are the basic units of inheritance, the means by which certain characteristics are passed on from parents to their offspring. One day, doctors may learn to change a child's genetic makeup before it is born. If they do, couples like David and Susan will be able to have children who are free of their families' inherited diseases.

But would it be right for such couples to seek to change their children's genetic structures? Or is the creation of new life a matter for God alone? Is it moral for doctors and scientists to experiment with genes and to meddle with human genetic inheritance?

Such questions have been in the news a great deal in recent months. So have questions like those about Billy and Mary. Today, the moral aspects of health care are of growing concern to Americans. The concerns range from genetic engineering to organ transplants, from the right to life to the right to die, from conflicts between medicine and religion to conflicts between medicine and money. They involve the rights of patients, medicine as a means of punishment, experimentation on human beings, and much more. Altogether, these concerns have been grouped under the term *bioethics*.

As a field, bioethics is only a few years old, but many bioethical questions date back to the beginning of medicine itself. Yet the questions are new, too, for today we must look at them in the light of twentieth-century medical technology and of modern social, religious, and political ideas.

Take the question of abortion. The oldest medical code of ethics, the Hippocratic oath, forbids doctors to perform the procedure. Physicians have respected the Hippocratic oath for 2400 years, since the Ancient Greek doctor Hippocrates is believed to have written it. But a majority of Americans today believe that each woman has the moral right to decide for herself whether or not to bear a child. Does that belief make abortion right?

Or take the matter of preserving life. For centuries doctors have felt this to be their highest duty. Today, though, dying men and women can be kept, sometimes despondent and in pain, on life-prolonging machines for weeks, even months. Must their lives be preserved, no matter what the suffering?

Bioethics seeks to help doctors, nurses, technicians, and other health care professionals (HCPs) deal with such dilemmas. It tries to help patients deal with them too. To do this, it must consider codes of medical ethics, such as the Hippocratic oath, by which HCPs have traditionally lived and practiced. Such codes deal primarily with personal and professional relationships between health professionals and the patients they treat. But bioethics covers far broader considerations as well.

Bioethics comprises every possible aspect of health care—medical, moral, social, political, religious, legal, and financial. It includes the questions raised by new biological research. It looks at the ways the results of that research may be used on patients. It includes a consideration of present ideas about personal freedom and human dignity. It scrutinizes outmoded laws and seeks to frame new ones. It deals with the enormous recent growth in available medical services in the United States and the tremendous cost of those services. Finally, it takes into account our views of ourselves as members of a humane and caring society.

The new-old questions of bioethics are being debated throughout the United States today. They are under discussion in operating rooms and in public health clinics, in medical and nursing schools, at doctors' conventions and in high school classrooms. They are being argued in the halls of Congress and in courts of law. They are being considered by hospital ethics committees, by the American Medical Association (the AMA is a professional organization of American doctors), by members of the clergy, and by concerned citizens. They are being analyzed at bioethical think tanks, like the Hastings Center, more formally known as the Institute of Society, Ethics and the Life Sciences, founded in 1969 at Hastings-on-Hudson, New York. During the late 1970s, several bioethical controversies were examined by a special commission appointed by United States President Jimmy Carter. The controversies are being discussed in books, magazines, and newspapers, and reported and dramatized on television.

But no matter where bioethics is talked about, the discussion cannot begin without a consideration of patients' rights.

2

The Rights of Patients

Mary E. Schloendorff entered New York Hospital in January 1908. She was complaining of stomach problems.

It was a Dr. Bartlett who first examined the woman. His diagnosis: a fibroid tumor. Dr. Bartlett reported this finding to the patient. On so much, everyone was agreed.

Then the stories began to diverge. Dr. Bartlett said that he told Mary Schloendorff that an operation was needed to remove the tumor. She agreed to undergo the procedure, and the tumor was promptly taken out.

The patient's story was different. According to her, Dr. Bartlett knew she did not want an operation so he informed her that he needed to examine her again, this time under anesthesia. She agreed to this second examination, and was etherized. When she awoke, however, she discovered that an operation had taken place.

Angered, Mary Schloendorff went to court, accusing Dr. Bartlett and New York Hospital of deceiving her and of operating without her permission. By 1914, the case had reached the Supreme Court of the state of New York.

After listening to arguments on both sides, the court found in favor of the patient. Justice Benjamin Cardozo summed up the majority opinion. "Every human being of adult years and sound mind," he wrote, "has a right to determine what should be done with his own body; and a surgeon who performs an operation without his patient's consent commits an assault, for which he is liable in damages." Cardozo meant that every patient has the right to decide for him- or herself whether or not to accept treatment. If treatment is given against a patient's will that treatment amounts to an assault—a physical attack—upon the patient.

Such an attack is a form of malpractice. Malpractice is professional misconduct by a health care professional, misconduct that the patient feels has been harmful to him or to her. If a doctor operates without the patient's permission, that's malpractice. A surgeon who botches an operation, an internist who prescribes the wrong drug, a doctor who sets a broken leg so that the person ends up with a limp—all could be guilty of malpractice. Each may have to repay the patient, in money, for the injury caused.

Naturally, health care professionals do not want their patients suing for malpractice. Therefore they and the administrators of the institutions at which they practice require each patient to sign a consent form before undergoing treatment. This protects the patient because it ensures that no procedure will be carried out without his or her permission. A signed consent form protects the hospital and the HCPs too. It is a sort of agreement in advance that the patient will not sue for malpractice.

For years consent forms did their job, and few malpractice suits were brought before American courts. Then, about twenty years ago, that began to change. More and more patients—even those who had signed consent forms—were charging malpractice.

Why? Medicine has changed in many ways since the early part of the century. With those developments has come a change in people's attitudes toward medical care and toward the men and women who provide it.

A Changing Medical World

Years ago, medicine could not accomplish what it can today. Early in this century doctors could not make the sophisticated diagnoses that are now routine. They lacked modern drugs and the surgical tools and techniques that are commonplace in the 1980s. But twentieth-century improvements in the quality of medical care have not improved the relations between doctor and patient. Often, they have done the reverse.

Early in the century, many doctors and patients knew each other better than most do today. People moved around less, and often stayed with just one physician for thirty or forty years. That one doctor treated them for everything. He was trusted and respected, perhaps even loved, by his patients.

It's a rare doctor and patient who have that kind of a relationship today. Most doctors now practice in groups. You may go to Dr. Smith for your regular checkups, but if Dr. Smith is off duty when you get flu, you'll have to see Dr. Brown. Next time you're sick, both Smith and Brown may be off duty. You'll end up seeing Dr. Jones. It is hard to build up a solid relationship with any one doctor under such circumstances.

When a person falls ill, complications increase. Serious illness requires a specialist. The patient with heart disease sees a cardiologist; one with cancer, an oncologist; one with a blood disorder, a hemotologist. Specialists are inevitable in today's complex and fast-changing medical world. New discoveries are made so frequently that no single doctor can keep up with them all. Each must specialize in a particular area.

Since that area can be extremely narrow, one specialist may not be enough. A patient hospitalized with a major illness may see one specialist in the morning and another, whose expertise is in a slightly different area, in the afternoon. Either or both may call in still other doctors. Soon the patient may be under the care of four or five different people, all of them strangers.

That makes it hard for patients to find out how ill they are, or how their conditions might be treated. Each doctor may assume that another specialist, or the patient's regular doctor, has clarified all the details. Or each may give the patient a slightly different explanation of what is going on. Either way, patients often feel confused and bewildered. Result: when they sign a consent form, they may be signing blindly, not really understanding what is to be done to them.

When that happens, unpleasant surprises are likely. One man may find that the drug he is taking has debilitating side effects no one warned him of. He accuses his doctor of malpractice. A woman may think she has agreed to exploratory surgery—and awake to find she has undergone a major amputation. She brings a malpractice suit. Some patients are simply disappointed that procedures do not turn out as well as expected. They too file for malpractice.

The growing number of malpractice suits alarmed HCPs. Some, convicted of delivering faulty care, had to pay hundreds of thousands of dollars in damages. Others tried to protect themselves by taking out malpractice insurance. That way, if they were found guilty of malpractice, the insurance companies would pay. But insurance executives were also alarmed by all the suits. They raised their rates so high that some doctors could not afford them. Doctors were beginning to find themselves in a predicament. How could they get out of it? Many decided the answer lay in the patients' rights movement.

A "Bill of Rights" for Patients

The patients' rights movement was new in the 1960s, but it caught on rapidly. Leaders of the movement included a number of HCPs as well as patients themselves. Their goal was to establish formal guidelines—a sort of "patients' bill of rights"—to define the relationship between patients and those who care for them. Such relationships, leaders of the movement believed, must be based on mutual respect. Not only must the patient respect the health professionals, but professionals must respect their patients. They must recognize patients as individual human beings with specific human needs and rights. It was that recognition that patients' rights activists sought to write into their guidelines.

An important milestone for the movement came in 1970. That year, the Joint Commission on the Accreditation of Hospitals put its weight behind the idea of a bill of rights for hospital patients. About 70 percent of this country's hospitals have commission accreditation. The group's 1970 action was to make adoption of a patients' bill of rights the first item on its list of standards. That meant no hospital could be accredited unless it had formally agreed to safeguard the rights of the people entrusted to its care.

Two years later, the American Hospital Association (AHA) took a similar action. Nearly all 7,000 American hospitals belong to the AHA. In 1972 the group drew up a twelve-point bill of rights and began urging its adoption.

The AHA document is very like the Joint Commission's. Both emphasize two areas of rights. First is the right to give consent—informed consent—to treatment. Each declaration stresses the responsibility of HCPs and institutions to be sure patients thoroughly understand their conditions and the recommended course of treatment. The second area addressed in each document is the patient's right to privacy.

Adoption of the bills was a triumph for the patients' rights movement. But it was only a first step. The next, making the rights a reality, is less easily accomplished.

In the first place, the AHA did no more than make a recommendation. The Joint Commission went further, making adoption of patients' rights a standard that must be met for accreditation. However, no hospital is required to meet the Commission's standards. It can be to an institution's advantage to be accredited, since the federal government will then automatically repay it for some of the costs of treating its elderly patients. An unaccredited hospital may have to wait for a special inspection before payment is made. Still, a hospital that does not want to bother with a bill of rights can simply forego accreditation.

A second problem is that even if a hospital has an official bill of rights, no outside agency checks to see how well it is enforced. Even when HCPs are sincerely committed to enforcing patients' rights, they may find it difficult to do so. In some cases, they may even decide enforcement is unethical. That is because the ethics of informed consent and the right to privacy turn out to be much more complex than they appear to be on the surface.

Informed Consent—Is It Always Possible?

Consider consent to treatment and the sheer amount of information patients need if their consent is to be truly informed.

If a disease is serious, its treatment is bound to be complicated. Even with the best intentions, doctors may not be able to make clear to patients exactly what they want to do.

At times the doctor may not fully understand a patient's condition and prospects. "Though anticoagulants, antibiotics, hypotensive agents, insulin, and steroids have been available for 15 to 40 years," writes one bioethicist, "many of their true effects are unknown . . . . [Doctors] are still uncertain about the best means of treatment for even such routine problems as a common cold, a sprained back, a fractured hip . . . ." How, then, can they be certain about the best way to treat a rare cancer or to use a potent new drug? How can they fully inform a patient about something they themselves may not really understand?

Another problem can be that HCPs who believe in obtaining informed consent in general may question the wisdom of doing so in a particular case. Suppose a doctor is dealing with a person who is highly suggestible. Tell this patient that he might experience a certain symptom, and he promptly does. Say that his medicine may cause nausea, and he quickly gets sick. Such reactions may slow his recovery—or prevent it altogether. Is it going to help him to learn all the symptoms he *could* develop, all the complications surgery *can* lead to, all the *possible* side effects of the drugs prescribed for him? Would it really be unethical to gloss over the truth a little?

Other considerations can cloud the issue. A sick woman who is depressed to begin with may sink into profound despair if a doctor says her illness could be fatal. Her despair may keep her from cooperating fully with the doctor. Should the doctor phrase the diagnosis differently—make it sound less serious? Should the doctor lie a little for the patient's own good?

Another patient may be depressed, depressed enough to refuse treatment outright. He may prefer to die quickly, avoiding months of the therapy that even his own doctor warns will be painful and expensive. Then the doctor has observed the patient's rights—and cost him his life. Some patients who are confronted with catastrophic diagnoses may kill themselves. How moral is it to observe a patient's right to be informed if it leads directly to his death?

Questions like these have no simple answers. Some doctors think it is ethical to withhold information in some cases. Being less than totally honest is moral, they say, when it helps the patient in the long run. To support such a view, doctors may quote the oldest of medical maxims: "First, do no harm." Sometimes, they contend, the way to avoid doing harm is to ignore a patient's so-called right to the truth.

Other doctors reject this idea. To them, concealing the truth is no different from telling a direct lie. Both are unethical because both deny patients their human right to make free choices based on full knowledge of the facts. Honesty may hurt some patients at first, but dishonesty is a lasting moral wrong.

If the issue of informed consent turns out to be more involved than it appears at first, so does the matter of privacy. This right, the second covered in most hospital guidelines, encompasses two distinct areas: physical privacy, and confidentiality—the right of patients to keep their personal and medical histories a secret between their doctors and themselves.

The Right to Privacy

In the past, physical privacy was not the issue it is today. Years ago, most patients were treated in the privacy of their own homes. Today, hospitalization is the rule. Many people in hospitals and other health-care facilities find physical privacy to be almost nonexistant.

In crowded institutions, it is virtually impossible for a patient to go alone into a room and close the door, confident of not being disturbed. In many places, several patients are jammed into a single room or forced to live together in large, barrackslike spaces. What goes on in one corner can be overheard and overseen from any other. At teaching hospitals, where medical students are trained, patients may have to undergo one examination after another as young doctors learn to "make the rounds."

Can anything be done about these invasions of privacy? Administrators at some institutions have placed limits on the number of examinations students may carry out on patients. Many HCPs have become more sensitive about providing a measure of privacy by placing screens around beds while examining or caring for patients. The patients' rights movement has been responsible for many such changes.

But the movement has not been able to do much to safeguard the other kind of privacy—the confidentiality of patient-doctor relations. Even as the movement was making it an issue, the last vestiges of confidentiality may have been vanishing from the American medical scene.

An End to Confidentiality

Patients must confide in their doctors. A doctor must know all a patient's symptoms, even the most intimate. He or she needs to know about other things too—drinking and smoking habits, diet and exercise patterns, whether the patient has irrational fears or deep depressions. Even the patient's sex life may be relevant to treatment.

Once, patients could trust doctors and other HCPs with such information. Most medical professionals deserved the trust. They valued their patients' privacy and felt a responsibility to respect their personal secrets.

Today, many do not. Tune into any TV soap opera, and you're sure to see "doctors" and "nurses" chatting freely about this or that "patient." The gossip is essential on TV— it's one way soap opera writers keep their plots thickening. The problem is that many real-life HCPs seem little different from their TV counterparts. "In too many hospitals," says a spokesperson for one Boston hospital, "rounds may be conducted in hallways or elevators." Administrators at that hospital have posted signs: "Hospital staff are reminded that patient information should not be discussed in public areas."

The gossip isn't confined to hospitals. Dr. Lawrence K. Altman, medical correspondent for *The New York Times*, recounts a disturbing experience aboard an Amtrak train. In one car a young doctor was telling a companion about some of his cases. Absorbed by what he was saying, he failed to notice how loudly he was speaking. Soon, everyone in the vicinity knew all about his patients—including their names. "Some doctors," Dr. Altman concludes, "no longer value confidentiality as highly as virtually all doctors once did."

Why not? Again, part of the answer goes back to some of the ways medicine has changed. Once doctors knew most of their patients as individuals with secrets that were important to them. Now a busy doctor has so many patients that it's hard to get to know them personally. To present-day doctors, patients may not be so much distinct personalities as they are a collection of fascinating symptoms needing to be treated. Patients are medical challenges, not private human beings.

Nor is careless talk· by doctors themselves the only threat to patient confidentiality. Our medical secrets are known to many—to doctors' receptionists, assistants, nurses, and billing clerks. The charts and records of hospital patients are open to many more: laboratory and x-ray technicians, dieticians, student doctors, residents and interns, three shifts of nurses and nurses' aides, volunteers, the men and women who program the computers in which hospital records are kept. According to the American College of Hospital Administrators, an average of seventy-five people in every major hospital have access to patient records. Any of these seventy-five people may spill a secret. If doctors cannot control their own gossiping, how can they expect to stop that of others?

But even if everyone with access to medical records were absolutely discreet, secrets would continue to leak out. Says Dr. Altman, "The insurance system alone has eliminated any remnant of confidentiality."

Other Threats to Confidentiality
Medical care in the United States is expensive, and only a multimillionaire could afford to pay for treatment of a long or serious illness. For the rest of us, paying our doctors' bills means relying on private medical insurance or such government funding programs as Medicare (for the elderly) or Medicaid (for the needy). No matter which patients turn to, their medical histories are opened up to another set of people.

Doctors are required to turn over their records to insurance companies upon request. This is reasonable. The companies have a right to know about the health of the people whose bills they pay. But how does opening the records affect the patient's right to privacy? If an insurance company finds out that someone has an alcohol problem, will his rates go up? His insurance be canceled? If he is insured through the place where he works, chances are his employer may learn about his alcoholism. Will that mean fewer promotions? The loss of his job?

When a person receives Medicaid or Medicare funds, the state or federal government gets into the act. Government inspectors, like insurance-company employees, may demand to view patient records. "What if Medicare finds out that you're a drug addict?" asks Robert Gelman, a lawyer for a congressional committee that has been studying the problem of disappearing patient confidentiality. "There's an incredible amount of information on everybody and we are losing control of it," Gelman warns.

Other factors threaten confidentiality. Government information about our health goes beyond Medicare and Medicaid records. In 1983, the federal Department of Health and Human Services adopted a "squeal rule." This rule applied to any federally funded clinic that gave out birth-control information. Under it, whenever such a clinic prescribed a birth-control method for a teenaged girl, it was required to inform the girl's parents. It's easy to see how the squeal rule got its name!

Although officials at Health and Human Services defended their rule as an excellent way to improve teenagers' morals and help family members to communicate better, most HCPs condemned it as an unethical attack upon the right to privacy. After nearly a year of fierce public debate, the government abandoned its controversial regulation.

The squeal rule may have been an inappropriate attempt to legislate teenagers' morals, but other rules that require HCPs to report on certain of their patients may have a more compelling justification. "The right of privacy is not absolute," ruled a California court in one health-related case, "and in some cases is subordinate to the state's fundamental right to enact laws which promote public health, welfare and safety."

When might the public welfare be at stake? Suppose a doctor is called in to examine a patient with a gunshot wound. By law the doctor must report that patient to the police. That is because the injury may be evidence that a crime has taken place. If it has, the state has a compelling interest in bringing the criminal to justice.

Yet some HCPs question the ethics of obeying laws that require them to report such wounds. If they do obey, what happens to their patients' right to privacy? Suppose a doctor in a hospital emergency room finds that a patient is carrying heroin packaged for sale? Should he report that? On the one hand, selling heroin is a crime that endangers members of the public. On the other, the patient, by appearing in the emergency room, has entrusted himself to the doctor. Must the doctor betray that trust?

Or the doctor in question could be a psychiatrist. If one of the doctor's patients says she is going to kill her husband, what should the doctor do? Report it to the police? Warn the husband? Assume that the wife isn't really serious—that she is merely venting her aggression in a harmless way? What if a patient speaks of killing the president of the United States?

There is another—and new—threat to patient privacy today. That threat is the computer.

In June 1983, a computer systems manager at one New York City hospital discovered a problem in the hospital's computerized records. A computer that had been monitoring therapy for 250 patients had failed. In addition, about $1,500 worth of billing records had been destroyed. It was clear that some computer "hacker" had learned the system's password and broken into it. Unless the culprit were caught, all the hospital's patient records could be at risk. Private information might be stolen from those records, or false information added.

The culprit was caught—that time. But what if other hackers gain access to other medical records? American medicine is relying more and more upon computers. In two New York City hospital clinics, for instance, computers are used to keep track of the pediatric care given to children in order to make that care more efficient. Dr. Richard K. Stone, chief of pediatrics at one of the hospitals, is enthusiastic about the program. "In one way,'" he says, "we are now looking over a doctor's shoulder with the help of a computer printout." Will the doctor be equally enthusiastic if unauthorized intruders also start peering over the doctor's shoulder? The threat that computer misuse poses to patient privacy is a bioethical issue that people in the medical community are just beginning to consider.

Where does all this—the disappearance of confidentiality, the problems of providing physical privacy, the dilemmas over informed consent—leave patients' rights? The good news is that the idea of patients' rights is now official policy at thousands of the institutions that care for the sick, the elderly, and the handicapped. The bad news is that, in the real world of practical, everyday considerations, many patients remain unable to truly enjoy those rights.

Both the good news and the bad are reflected in the most recent code of the American Medical Association. That code, adopted in 1981, instructs the physician to "respect the rights of patients." For the first time ever, the AMA has officially acknowledged that patients do have certain rights that need to be specifically spelled out. But the group's code continues to leave it up to each doctor to work out how—and how effectively—he or she will observe those rights.

3

Organs for Sale

The ad appeared in the December 25, 1983, edition of the Burlington County, New Jersey, *Times*:

> KIDNEY FOR SALE—From 32 yr.
> old Caucasian female in excellent
> health. Write to PO Box---, -----------,
> NJ 085--.

Bizarre as this ad may seem, it was not the only one of its kind to appear that year. In Georgia, a man named Harold Hedrick was offering to sell a kidney for $25,000. He wanted the money to buy a fast-food restaurant. A woman in the same state was trying to sell one of her kidneys to a medical college for a bargain price—just $5,000. Less generously, some Californians were said to be offering their organs for up to $160,000. And in Reston, Virginia, Dr. H. Barry Jacobs was proposing to turn the buying and selling of kidneys into a regular business.

Dr. Jacobs called his business idea International Kidney Exchange. As he explained it, he would be providing a vital service to desperately ill men, women, and children.

Thousands of Americans suffer from serious diseases of the kidney. The kidneys' function is to separate toxic, or poisonous wastes out of the blood. Then these wastes are eliminated through the urinary tract.

Healthy kidneys do their job efficiently. In fact, although people are normally born with two kidneys, one alone is generally capable of cleansing the bloodstream. So if a single kidney is damaged or destroyed—or sold—a person's health is not likely to be seriously affected. However, if both kidneys are damaged, by accident or illness, it's a different story. Wastes build up and illness develops.

If the illness becomes severe enough, the patient may have to rely upon an artificial-kidney machine. This device works outside the body. A catheter, a hollow needle, is inserted into an artery in the patient's arm, and blood is drawn through it into the machine. There, wastes are taken out, and the blood passes back into the patient's body. Over and over, this process—known as kidney dialysis—is repeated. When all the wastes have been removed, the machine is turned off and the patient disconnected from it. About 70,000 Americans with kidney disease depend upon dialysis to live.

But although dialysis can be a life-saver, it is an expensive one. It costs about $2 billion a year to dialyze all those Americans who need the procedure. Thanks to the efforts of the National Kidney Foundation, a group that works on behalf of kidney patients, much of this bill is paid by the federal government.

Kidney dialysis is also extremely time-consuming. Each session lasts several hours, and the average patient must be hooked up to the machine two or three times a week. Not surprisingly, thousands of men, women, and children with kidney disease would like to find an alternative to dialysis.

An alternative exists. It is a kidney transplant. For over twenty years, doctors have known how to replace diseased kidneys with a healthy organ from a human donor. The first experimental human kidney transplant operation was performed in 1960. Today the procedure is almost routine. Perhaps the greatest difficulty about it lies in finding organs suitable for transplanting.

The Organ Shortfall

One source is the body of a person who has just died. Hospitals allow doctors to take organs from cadavers, provided the dead person has earlier given permission for this to be done. Sometimes a dead person's surviving relatives may grant permission. Unfortunately, however, permission may not be easy to get. Many people are unwilling to allow their own organs or those of family members to be used for transplants. Others are unaware of the need for donors. Even when permission is given, a person may have died in a way that leaves the kidneys too badly damaged to be usable. Another difficulty is that for a transplant to be successful, donor and recipient must be closely "matched" according to various chemical factors. A recipient's body will quickly reject any organ that is not a good match.

Transplantable kidneys may also come from living donors. Living donors, of course, must prepare to go through the rest of their lives with a single kidney. That is one reason why there are so few of them. True, one healthy kidney seems able to do its job as well as two. But what if a donor's remaining kidney is later damaged or destroyed? Where does that leave the donor?

People may be reluctant to volunteer as donors for other reasons. The kidney-removal operation is unpleasant and painful. Furthermore, any operation—even the most routine—places the patient at some risk. Only a close relative, a parent, or a brother or sister, is likely to offer a kidney to a dying patient.

The difficulties in obtaining kidneys suitable for transplanting cause a serious shortfall. Of the 10,000 or so Americans who need transplants in any given year, only slightly over 5,000 will get them.

It was to try to close the gap between supply and demand that Dr. Jacobs founded International Kidney Exchange in 1983. To him, the shortfall problem was simple, a problem that could be solved by dollars and cents. Voluntary efforts weren't producing nearly enough kidneys? Very well. He would obtain kidneys—at a price—from people around the world. Then he would sell the organs—at a higher price—to people who were waiting for them. After all, Dr. Jacobs pointed out, no state or federal law forbade the sale of body parts for transplants. "Where is the wind blowing?" he demanded. Clearly, it was not blowing in the direction of voluntary donations. The doctor answered his own question: "It is the money wind."

Dr. Jacobs soon realized that International Kidney Exchange was not likely to blow any money his way. The president of the National Kidney Foundation, Dr. David A. Ogden, quickly denounced the plan as "immoral and unethical." Other doctors reacted the same way. It is wrong to exchange living human organs for cash, they said. It is immoral to use money to tempt people to submit to a major operation and to deprive them of a vital organ. Even worse, what if some of the people tempted by money decided to make a little extra by selling their children's kidneys? What if they went on having more and more children in hope of adding to the family income?

Other objections were raised. The people selling their kidneys would be from the poorer nations of Asia, Africa, and Latin America. Most of those buying would be from a rich country, the United States. Is it ethical to ask the poor to jeopardize their health to guarantee the health of the rich?

Doctors were not alone in condemning International Kidney Exchange. There was concern in the United States Congress too.

Albert Gore, Jr., then a representative from Tennessee, spoke against the plan. "People should not be regarded as things to be bought and sold like parts of an automobile," he told a group of news reporters. In October 1983, Gore introduced a bill in the House of Representatives that called for making it a crime to buy or sell any human organ. Several other senators and representatives introduced or sponsored similar bills.

A year later, none of these bills had yet become law. If any do, they will do more than make the buying and selling of organs illegal. They will also establish a national clearing house for organ transplants. Computers there will link hospitals around the country so that donors and recipients can be matched as quickly and efficiently as possible.

In addition, enactment of such bills would force each state to adopt a uniform program of funding for organ-transplant operations. Organs to be covered under the bills would include hearts, lungs, and livers, as well as kidneys. All have been successfully transplanted in human beings.

Forcing each state to establish a rigid funding program seems especially important to bioethicists. As of mid-1984, no one could predict which patients would be able to afford an operation and which would not.

Transplants and Political Pull

Sara Brookwood, a young Massachusetts woman, thought money was no problem for her. She needed a new liver, and since her private insurance company had refused to pay the $180,000 bill, Massachusetts Medicaid officials had agreed to do so. (Medicaid programs in each of the fifty states help provide medical care for those who cannot afford it.) But in 1982 when Sara was on a plane headed for the out-of-state hospital where the transplant would take place, officials changed their minds. Massachusetts Medicaid would not foot Sara's bill after all.

Others have found themselves in Sara's position. Some private insurance companies pay for organ transplants; others do not. Some pay for some transplants—livers, for instance—but not for others. The Medicaid situation is equally snarled. Since each state administers its own Medicaid program, each has its own set of rules. In 1984, twenty-nine state Medicaid programs refused to pay for heart or liver transplants. Three states paid for liver transplants, but not heart transplants. Fourteen had agreed to consider payment on a case-by-case basis. The four remaining states had no policy at all.

But that's not the end of the confusion. Some people do get Medicaid to pay for their operations, even when their state's program does not regularly cover transplant costs. Sara Brookwood was one of them.

Sara's father, Myron Teichholtz, knew someone who worked as an aide to President Ronald Reagan. The minute Teichholtz got word of Medicaid's decision not to pay for his daughter's surgery, he was on the phone to the White House. His political connection paid off. The presidential aide telephoned the governor of Massachusetts, Edward J. King. If Governor King did not convince Medicaid officials to reverse their decision once more, the aide warned him, Teichholtz would take out a full-page ad in a leading Boston newspaper the next day. "The governor of Massachusetts is responsible for my daughter's death . . ." the ad would announce in bold, black headlines.

Massachusetts Medicaid agreed to pay for Sara Brookwood's operation.

Sara's story is not unique. Another Massachusetts father, Charles Fiske, turned to elected officials and the news media in an effort to win private insurance funding when his daughter needed a liver transplant in 1982. Like Teichholtz, Fiske got the money. (Fiske was more fortunate than the other man, however. His daughter, Jamie, survived. Sara Brookwood's doctors could not find a suitable donor for her, and she died.)

In several instances, the anguished families of patients needing transplants have turned for help to the nation's highest political figure, the president. In 1983, President Reagan appealed on radio for a donor for an eleven-month-old Texas girl with a diseased liver. The girl's family was grateful, but still more help was needed. Texas Medicaid does not pay for liver transplants. No doubt feeling that the White House was watching, Texas legislators acted quickly. They passed a special bill providing payment for this liver transplant—*and for no other.* President Reagan has involved himself in obtaining special help for other potential transplant patients as well. Nevertheless, he opposed the idea of routine Medicaid funding for transplant operations, claiming that such funding would cost too much.

Naturally, no one is sorry to see someone step in to try to save the life of a child or a young woman—or anyone else. But many people do deplore the necessity for it. Private insurors should have a firm, established policy regarding payments for transplants, they say. So should Medicaid. A person's ability to obtain an operation should not have to depend upon the political support his or her family can muster.

Other Ethical Questions

Although the bills presented in Congress in 1983 attempted to deal with some of the ethical questions involved in organ transplants, they left many others unresolved. For instance, in the case of donations from cadavers, there is the problem of deciding just when to take an organ, even if permission has been granted. As we will see in Chapter 9, doctors have found it increasingly difficult to determine exactly when a person really is finally and irrevocably dead. Respirators and other machines can keep a person "breathing" and his or her blood "flowing" long after the body has ceased to function on its own.

Yet kidneys, liver, and other organs may deteriorate while a patient is on life-support systems. By the time a person is at last declared dead, the organs may no longer be useful. Should a twenty-year-old with liver disease be allowed to die while a potential donor, eighty years old and in a coma, "lives" on, unknowing and uncaring? On the other hand, could the demand for healthy, living kidneys, livers, hearts, and lungs lead some doctors to pronounce patients dead prematurely?

A different set of moral questions is involved when the organs come from living donors. Some give freely and joyfully; others do not. "After I give her the damned kidney, I never want to see her again," one woman said bitterly as she prepared to donate an organ to her dying sister. Even people who seem to be willing donors may have hidden resentments and reservations. They may feel they have been unfairly pressured into making the sacrifice. Some may have been emotionally blackmailed by other family members into trying to save the life of a relative. For such reasons, many surgeons believe it is unethical to transplant kidneys from living donors under any circumstances.

Other ethical problems crop up. If three kidney patients are dying, and only one suitable organ is available, which patient should get it? How should the choice be made? On the basis of age? Intelligence? Character? On the number of children each patient has? The social usefulness of each one's job? The ability of each to pay? *Who* should make the choice? So far, no one has come up with satisfactory answers to such questions, but at least the questions are being debated, not ignored.

4

Medicine in the Courtroom

The cubicle looked like a sparsely equipped hospital room: bright lights overhead, a freshly made-up cot on wheels, intravenous (IV) tubes—even a curtain for privacy. The patient, too, appeared to be quite ordinary. A forty-year-old man named Charlie Brooks, Jr., entered the room and sat down, then stretched out on the cot. He said a short prayer, as anyone facing a major medical procedure might. A technician inserted an IV catheter into each of Brooks's arms and a saline (salt) solution began dripping into his body. Not far away, a physician, Dr. Ralph Gray, waited, prepared to help out if needed.

Needed to do what? What miracle of healing was going on in that small room in Texas on December 7, 1982?

None. The scene was one of death, not life. Dr. Gray was not there to cure, but to monitor a killing. Charlie Brooks, convicted murderer, was being executed.

As Brooks lay strapped to the cot, the technician added sodium pentothal, an anesthesia used in surgery, to the saline solution. Brooks yawned. More sodium pentothal—five times the normal anesthetic dose—flowed into his body. Brooks slept and died. Just to make sure, though, the executioner added two more drugs, a paralytic agent and one that interferes with heart action, to the IV bag. Minutes later, Brooks was officially declared dead, the first person executed by lethal injection in the United States.

The first, but not the last. Within months, there was another execution by lethal injection in Texas and one in North Carolina. Of the thirty-eight states that permitted capital punishment in 1984, twelve had authorized it by means of lethal injection. To many lawmakers, this form of execution seems kinder, more humane, than any other.

They may or may not be right. In October 1983, a Washington, D.C., court ordered an investigation into charges backed by what it called "substantial and uncontroverted evidence" that lethal injections can cause agonizingly painful death. Eighteen months later, the U.S. Supreme Court rejected efforts to outlaw lethal injections as a means of execution.

Of course, a great many people argue that all capital punishment is inhumane, no matter how the sentence is carried out. Lethal injection may be physically less messy or repulsive than executions by electrocution, hanging, or firing squad, they say, but it imposes the same mental agony on the condemned person. Leaving aside the debate over the death penalty itself, however, execution by lethal injection poses a special problem for medicine.

Medicine and Lethal Injections

Offically, the AMA condemns the participation of doctors in executions. Helping out at an execution is a direct violation of the physician's sworn obligation to save life, the association has ruled. How, then, could Dr. Gray have taken part in Brooks's death?

The doctor's answer is simple. He did not take part in the execution. He bears no responsibility for it.

Dr. Gray and those who share his view point out that no death-penalty law requires a doctor to be the one to perform the execution. The physician's only duty is to keep an eye on the proceedings and to give advice if necessary. Thus, Dr. Gray examined Brooks's veins to make sure they were prominent enough for the IV needles to go in easily. No doubt he spoke with the executioner ahead of time, giving him pointers about how to do the insertions. But Dr. Gray himself did not touch the needles. He did not start the IV. He did not add the drugs to the saline solution. The doctor only checked a man's veins.

In the words of one Texas law enforcement officer, "Looking for veins doesn't count."

Doesn't count? Others wonder. If the executioner had not been able to find veins prominent enough to take the IV needles, he could not have put the needles in place. Even professional nurses and technicians sometimes have difficulty locating a vein from which they can draw sufficient blood for routine tests. Without the needles, there could have been no injection. No injection, no death. Dr. Gray did not perform the act that killed Charlie Brooks, but he did help to make that act go smoothly. Unlike a hanging or an electrocution, where a doctor might be asked only to pronounce a person dead, lethal injections require cooperation from a doctor ahead of time. That is one reason why this form of execution is a bioethical issue.

Another is that under slightly different circumstances a doctor's role could have been much more active than Dr. Gray's was. If Brooks had struggled, it might have taken a physician's skill to insert the needles properly. Other factors could have required his intervention. It can be difficult to set up an IV for anyone who has fragile veins or who is obese or very nervous. The technician who tries to execute such a person could cause terrible pain. If that happens, should the doctor step in, stop the executioner, and finish the job?

How would the AMA react if a doctor did do that? It is hard to predict, because for practical purposes, the group's position is more ambiguous than its official policy makes it appear. "The doctor may be forced to load the pistol," explains Samuel Sherman, vice-chairman of the AMA Judicial Council, "but he must never be the one to pull the trigger." People concerned with medicine's role in capital punishment note that unless the pistol is loaded, pulling the trigger won't hurt anyone.

Furthermore, Sherman's statement ignored the fact that somewhere, someday, someone who was nervous, or overweight, or who had delicate veins, or who was fighting to stay alive was probably going to face IV needles in a death chamber.

In March 1985, something like that happened in a Texas prison. It took a technician forty minutes to insert a needle into the right arm of a convicted killer. First, the technician tried the left arm, then the right, then the left again. Then he tried the legs. The problem: the convict's veins were all but destroyed, probably as a result of his drug habit. What was the attending physician's moral duty to this man?

This is a question the medical community will have to answer if the use of lethal injections continues in the United States. HCPs will have to draw up ethical guidelines regarding the use of medicine in some noncapital cases, as well.

Medical Treatment—or Jail

One place medicine is being used to help control crime is in St. Louis, Missouri. Some habitual drunk drivers in that city are being sentenced to undergo medical treatment. The treatment involves the drug tetraethylthiuram disulfide, more commonly known by its trade name, Antabuse.

Antabuse changes the way the body's metabolism reacts to alcohol. Instead of feeling pleasantly euphoric or relaxed, the drinker who has received a dose of Antabuse rapidly develops the symptoms of a monumental hangover: a feeling of being hot or flushed, a throbbing headache, violent nausea. Even a tiny amount of alcohol, such as that found in some cold medicines or which may be breathed in from varnish or certain cosmetics, can trigger the reaction.

Taking Antabuse makes it impossible for an alcoholic to drink—or at least, to drink and drive. It keeps intoxicated drivers off the roads as surely as jail does. Knowing this, one St. Louis judge offers men and women with several drunk driving convictions a choice: prison—or four years of Antabuse treatment. The doses are given under court order so that those sentenced to get them cannot cheat.

In other places, too, medicine has been used to fight crime. In a 1983 South Carolina case, three men were convicted of raping a young woman. The judge, C. Victor Pyle, Jr., directed each man to choose between thirty years in jail and freedom.

The condition for being set free, he added, would be to submit to an operation called bilateral orchidectomy. A bilateral orchidectomy is surgical castration.

That was the first time an American judge ever made surgical castration a part of a sentence handed down from the bench. It was not, however, the first instance of court-approved castration for men convicted of rape or of related offenses. In 1975, two California men convicted of child molestation requested a court there to permit them to undergo orchidectomies.

The men had been convicted two years earlier. At that time, they were committed to a state mental hospital. After nine months, however, doctors saw no improvement in their conditions. The men remained deeply troubled and, in the doctors' opinions, continued to be "dangerous to society." Since there seemed little hope they would ever recover, they were sent back to court for criminal sentencing.

The sentences were harsh—indeterminate terms in jail. That meant the men would stay in prison until someone decided it was safe to let them out. But doctors had already testified that it would probably never be safe. In effect, the men had been given life terms.

That is why they requested orchidectomies. Castrated, they stood a good chance of being set free. (In previous years, California courts had released a number of other sex offenders after castration.) The men signed waivers releasing their lawyers and the judge from responsibility for the operations. Other waivers protected the surgeon who had agreed to perform the orchidectomies from any malpractice suit.

The Ethics of Medical Punishments

Judges and others who favor castration for sex offenders see it as a wise and humane use of the art of medicine. For one thing, they say, it would not be used in every case, but only when doctors agree there is little hope that the offender will change. Nor is surgical castration completely irreversible. According to doctors, some of its effects may be overcome with doses of male hormones. Furthermore, sentencing someone to be castrated, like sentencing a dangerous alcoholic driver to Antabuse treatments, keeps the person out of jail and offers the chance to lead a productive life. Both methods show how medicine can be employed for a socially useful purpose.

Or so some think. Others are unconvinced. Medicine's duty is to serve the patient, they say, not the law. If medicine is to become a tool of punishment, decisions about treatment will be made on the basis of what seems best for the law, not on what is best for the patient. What is more, those decisions will be made by judges, not by qualified HCPs. The result could be doctors and other medical professionals practicing medicine against the best interests of those they are treating.

The director of one alcoholic detoxification center, for instance, worries about putting alcoholics on a drug as powerful as Antabuse without first giving them thorough psychiatric evaluations. A person with suicidal tendencies might deliberately combine Antabuse and alcohol with fatal consequences, he warns. This critic also points out that while Antabuse can help an alcoholic stop drinking, it can only do so over the long run if it is part of a rehabilitation program that includes psychiatric counseling. Using Antabuse alone is treating the alcoholic's symptom—drinking too much—without attacking the disease—alcoholism—itself. Finally, there is the question of whether or not Antabuse is the best drug to use. At least one other equally effective, but less powerful, drug is available. It might well be the treatment of choice in many cases.

Naturally, you couldn't expect a judge to know all that. Judges are well-versed in the law, but few have had medical training. Doctors and other HCPs who perform procedures and administer drugs on a judge's orders may be practicing very poor medicine.

Even dangerous medicine. Consider the three South Carolina men asked to choose between thirty years in jail and castration. If the charges against them were true, the three are brutally violent. Judge Pyle himself described their crime as the most "horrible" incident of rape he had heard in his career. Not only did the men apparently rape their victim repeatedly, but prosecutors contended that they also held her prisoner for six hours and tortured her throughout that time. Castrating a man may keep him from raping another woman. But will it keep him from kidnapping and torturing?

Most experts agree that rape is a crime of violence, anyway, not a crime of sex. It is unlikely that being forced to submit to castration will make these men any less violent than they are. "In fact," says the executive director of one South Carolina Rape Crisis Center, "there is the potential that they are going to be even more dangerous after they are castrated." Any doctor who does an orchidectomy on such men will be doing little to help them. He or she may even be setting the stage for future "horrible" outrages.

Judge Pyle was aware of the furor his sentence awakened, and before long, he responded to it. Perhaps, he said, the convicted men would agree to chemical, rather than surgical, castration. Chemical castration is produced with regular doses of Depo-provera, a female hormone. Men who receive shots of it experience various physical changes, including a diminished sex drive. Depo-provera has been used with rapists and other sex offenders in several parts of the country.

Are judges who prescribe Depo-provera practicing better medicine than those who order surgical castration? Many think so, if only because hormone treatments can be stopped at any time. Others, like Dr. Clifford M. Snapper of New York City, disagree. "I would like to tell the judge [in one case] of some of the potential dangers of Depo-provera," Dr. Snapper wrote in a letter to *The New York Times.* "Potentially fatal clots . . . and allergic reactions . . . in addition to various adverse gastrointestinal and psychiatric effects. The drug's effects . . . are totally unpredictable and its use in this context is contrary to the manufacturer's and health profession's intent."

Medical Punishment and Patients' Rights

There are other objections to allowing medicine to lend itself to the punishment of crime. One is that it cancels the patient's right to privacy. Suppose a person who has been sentenced to medical treatment decides to make a real effort to change. Making that change will require intense cooperation between the patient and the HCP assigned to give treatment. That cooperation can be built only on mutual trust and respect. But is it ethical for an HCP to encourage the patient to be honest if everything that passes between the two may have to be repeated in court? On the other hand, is it ethical to treat patients *without* encouraging them to try to get better?

Another question is whether or not medicine-as-punishment infringes upon a patient's right to give informed consent to treatment. Those who favor sentencing criminals to medical treatment maintain that there is no conflict. Judge Pyle, for one, believes that the rapists he instructed to decide between jail and castration have complete freedom to make up their minds what to do. "They can go to prison if they choose," he says.

The St. Louis judge who sentences drunk drivers to Antabuse agrees. No one forces treatment on these people. On the contrary, convicted criminals have been known to ask for treatment of their own accord. The two California child molesters did, and so have other sex offenders in that state. At Johns Hopkins University Hospital in Baltimore, about seventy-five sex criminals are voluntarily receiving Depo-provera shots. Similar programs have attracted sex offenders in other states.

Yet are the men really in the programs of their own free will? Do the South Carolina rapists have the freedom Judge Pyle claims? Were the California men free not to request orchidectomies? Is a drunk driver free to turn down Antabuse treatments?

Many medical and legal experts say the answer to each question is no. The stakes are too heavily weighted—Depo-provera or decades behind bars; orchidectomy or life imprisonment; Antabuse or months away from home and family. Threatening a person with jail makes a mockery of his or her legal right to give informed consent to treatment.

Some medical punishments may even be a violation of the U.S. Constitution. In 1985 the South Carolina Supreme Court ruled that castrating a rapist amounts to a "cruel and unusual" punishment. Such a punishment is forbidden under the Constitution's Bill of Rights. The South Carolina justices ordered the three men convicted in Judge Pyle's courtroom to begin serving thirty-year jail terms.

Yet there is another side to the ethical coin. Is it right to withhold treatments from prisoners who request them? The surgeon who agreed to castrate the California child molesters changed his mind after consulting with various state medical groups. Despite the signed malpractice waivers, the doctor learned he still might be subject to a lawsuit. Understandably, he refused to operate. The two men, unable to get the treatment they need in order to win their freedom, remain in jail. It seems clear that they were denied their right to give informed consent to treatment. But when? In 1975, when they originally agreed to undergo orchidectomies? Or now, when they cannot get them?

Does it matter anyway? Many people say that those who have committed vicious crimes do not deserve to have their medical rights so scrupulously respected. Molesting, raping, murdering, driving to endanger, they have violated the rights of others—and forfeited their own.

People who think this way have a point. Convicts are routinely denied many of the rights others enjoy—the right to physical freedom, to vote, to hold public office, perhaps the right to drive a car or to own a gun. So why should their medical rights be preserved? Why shouldn't medicine be used to punish and control them—even to kill them?

But the bioethical question goes beyond what criminals deserve—or what they don't. The bioethical question involves medicine itself—medicine, whose chief aim has always been to heal and to help. Can medicine fulfill that aim—and also serve as an instrument of retribution?

5

Bioethics and Human
Experimentation

On December 1, 1982, a dentist from Des Moines, Washington, became the first human being to have an artificial heart implanted in his chest. The dentist's name was Barney Clark, and the operation was performed at the University of Utah Medical Center.

Dr. Clark's new heart, constructed of plastic and held together with strips of Velcro, was linked to two tubes, also made of plastic. The six-foot-long tubes exited from Dr. Clark's body just under his ribs. At the other end, each was connected to an electric pump. As the pump operated, air pressure inside the tubes increased and decreased regularly. Each pressure change produced a heartbeat.

In all, that artificial heart beat more than 12 million times, keeping Dr. Clark alive for four months. He died on March 23, 1983, a victim of kidney failure, breathing problems, complete loss of blood pressure, and various other ailments. Possibly, he was also a victim of unethical human experimentation.

For the artificial heart was an experiment. Called the Jarvik-7 after its inventor, Dr. Robert Jarvik, its implantation in Dr. Clark's chest was just one step in a long-term scientific research project. Was it a step that should have been taken?

Before the operation, many people thought it should. Dr. Clark and his family did. His doctors, Jarvik and the surgeon who performed the operation, William DeVries, agreed. So did the hospital's Institutional Review Board (IRB), a sixteen-member committee of doctors, nurses, pharmacists, lawyers, philosophers, and laypeople. An IRB must approve any medical experiment on a human being before it can take place.

After Dr. Clark's death, however, attitudes changed. During 1983, the Utah hospital's IRB was asked to give permission for other artificial heart operations. For over a year, all requests were turned down. Not until June 1984 did the IRB decide to allow a second artificial heart implant.

Before that operation could be carried out in Utah, however, Dr. DeVries moved to a hospital in Louisville, Kentucky. There, late in 1984, he implanted an artificial heart into the chest of a middle-aged man named William Schroeder. Several months later, Schroeder was still alive. Other artificial heart implants followed. Also in 1984, in another daring procedure, doctors in California transplanted the heart of a baboon into a newborn infant. The child, known to the public only as "Baby Fae," survived three weeks with the animal heart. The new operations helped fuel the national debate over the ethics of such experimentation.

Must We Experiment on Human Beings?
Few would deny that controlled scientific experimentation on selected human beings is essential to medicine. How else can doctors and scientists test new drugs, new procedures? On animals? It is true that early models of the Jarvik heart were tested on animals before an artificial heart was implanted in Dr. Clark. But animal experiments are useful only up to a point. Animals are not subject to many of the diseases that plague us humans, so some conditions cannot be reproduced in dogs, rats, guinea pigs, and the like. In addition, animals sometimes react differently to certain drugs and procedures than people do. Experiments on animals are a vital first step in medical research. But United States law demands clinical testing in human beings before a drug or technique is approved for general use.

Human experimentation falls into three categories. First are experiments that the researcher carries out on him- or herself. One classic of this kind was conducted over a century ago by a scientist keen to disprove the then-new idea that germs can cause disease. To make his point, the scientist swallowed a beakerful of cholera germs. Luckily for him, he apparently had a natural immunity to cholera. He did not become ill.

In the second category are experiments carried out on the sick in the belief that the experiment will help them, or on the healthy in the belief that it will keep them well. The famous rabies experiment of the French scientist Louis Pasteur falls into this class. In 1885, a distraught mother brought her nine-year-old son to Dr. Pasteur. The boy had been bitten by a rabid dog, and the mother had heard that Pasteur had developed a vaccine that prevented rabies in dogs. Would he administer it to her son? Pasteur hesitated, then did as the mother asked. The boy survived.

The third group of experiments are those conducted on sick or healthy people with no intention of helping those people directly. Such experiments are done to gain information that may be used to help others at a later time. Most new-product testing by drug-manufacturing companies falls into this category.

Unethical Experimentation

Although there is broad public concern about the ethics of human experimentation today, this was not always the case. Nor have ethical considerations always been uppermost in the minds of researchers. During the 1930s, for instance, American doctors in the United States Public Health Service studied a group of black men in Tuskegee, Alabama. The men were suffering from syphilis, the most devastating of venereal diseases.

At that time, doctors had ways of treating syphilis, but no cure for it. The idea of the Health Service doctors was to test the effectiveness of the most common of these treatments by comparing the progress of treated patients with that of a group of men who received no treatment at all. Over the years, they watched the untreated men go through the successive stages of syphilis—heart and organ damage, degeneration of the central nervous system, blindness, insanity.

The Tuskegee experiment was unethical on several grounds. The men who were its subjects were not told about it and so had no chance to withdraw. Since they did not realize they were not getting treatment, it did not occur to them to seek medical care elsewhere. The fact that in the 1930s any such treatment would not have been very effective does not excuse the deception practiced by the Health Service doctors.

Unethical as the Tuskegee experiments were, they could not compare to the "experiments" carried out in the prison camps of Nazi Germany before and during World War II. Actually, these were not experiments at all—merely tortures. Many of them, however, were dreamed up by a doctor, Josef Mengele, who claimed that what he was doing was scientifically valid. His "experiments" consisted of subjecting people to extremes of temperature, observing them starve to death, seeing how they reacted to unnecessary operations without anesthesia, and so on.

With the defeat of Nazi Germany in 1945 came worldwide awareness of what had gone on in the death camps and a determination to see that nothing like it ever happened again. At international conferences in 1948, 1964, and 1975, codes of ethics for human experimentation were debated, adopted, and amended. Chief among their provisions was that human experimental subjects must voluntarily agree to participate. Their agreement must come after they have been fully informed about the purpose, nature, and duration of the experiment, and about its risks and benefits to themselves.

Despite the new codes, however, abuses persisted in many countries, including the United States. In 1963, Americans learned that elderly patients at the Jewish Chronic Disease Hospital in Brooklyn, New York, had been injected with live cancer cells. That experiment was done under the auspices of the Sloan-Kettering Memorial Cancer Center, considered one the nation's most distinguished hospitals. The patients experimented upon were senile—unable to understand what the doctors were doing to them or to object to it.

Other experiments were conducted between 1956 and 1970 at the Willowbrook state hospital for the mentally retarded in New York. There, children were deliberately infected with hepatitis, a disease of the liver. The doctors who designed this experiment professed a worthwhile purpose—trying to develop a hepatitis vaccine. But their methods were strikingly unethical. Their subjects were mentally incompetent, under the age of legal consent, and inmates of an institution they were not free to leave.

Alarmed by reports like these, the Public Health Service took action. In the mid-1960s, it announced human experimentation guidelines for any research that receives funding from the federal government. This would include most hospital and university research, since such institutions receive frequent U.S. government grants. In 1974, the Health Service guidelines became official policy.

The guidelines require the informed consent of all human research subjects. They also mandate the establishment of Institutional Review Boards at hospitals that permit any human research. About 550 IRBs, including the one that approved Dr. Clark's operation, presently function in the United States.

In that same year, 1974, Congress took action of its own. It passed the National Research Act, which in turn established the National Commission for the Protection of Human Subjects of Biomedical and Behavioral Research. Between 1975 and 1978, the commission published recommendations to guarantee the rights of research subjects. Under the provisions of the 1974 act, the Department of Health and Human Services was required to adopt these recommendations (or other, equally strong, ones). Bioethical considerations were becoming official regulation.

Yet abiding by the regulations has proved difficult. Just as adopting a patients' bill of rights is easier than enforcing it, following strict rules in human research is easier said than done.

The Risks and Benefits of Human Experimentation

One problem lies in assessing the risks and benefits a proposed experiment holds for a subject. In the case of the first artifical heart implant for example, the IRB had to decide whether the risk to Dr. Clark was balanced by the possible benefit.

On one level, it was a simple equation. Barney Clark was dying. Only an artifical heart could keep him alive. But the

IRB had to consider more than life versus death. It had to take into account the quality of the life Dr. Clark would lead if he lived.

In many ways, that quality was poor. After the operation, Dr. Clark suffered serious nosebleeds and life-threatening convulsions. He was confused at times and was never considered remotely well enough to leave the hospital. Even if he had gone home, he would have remained tethered to a 375-pound machine for life.

But the quality of a person's life is not so easy to judge. Life is life, even bound to a machine. And Dr. Clark went through periods when he was not confused, not bleeding, not convulsing. He got to spend time with his family during his "extra" four months of life. He enjoyed TV football.

Besides considering risks and benefits to the subject, an IRB must look at the risk to the individual versus the possible benefits to society as a whole. In the case of the experiment on Dr. Clark, the benefits to society could prove substantial. Dr. DeVries and his team learned a lot from the dentist from Washington, information that they put to use two years later in Louisville. If someday artificial hearts begin saving thousands of lives, it will be thanks in part to his courage. Dr. Clark knew that. "If I can make a contribution, my life will count for something," he said as he prepared to undergo the operation. Yet that contribution came at the price of great suffering.

Which should an IRB give more weight to as it threads its way through risks and benefits, individuals or society? To some, society's needs are paramount. "We have a responsibility to future generations as well as to our present patients," says one British doctor. "It is unethical not to experiment on our patients."

Others disagree. Even if by injuring or killing just a few, doctors could find a cure for cancer, they say, doing so would be immoral.

In considering risks and benefits, an IRB must also consider the competence of the researcher whose project it is debating. The risk to a human subject can be increased if the experiment is poorly planned, inadequately prepared for, or carelessly conducted. The IRB at the University of Utah has been criticized, for example, because it allowed the Clark operation before the Jarvik-7 had been tested on any sick animals. The fact that doctors knew only how the heart worked in healthy bodies may have placed the critically ill Dr. Clark at greater risk than he otherwise would have been.

The federal government too may be neglecting to safeguard human subjects. A report released by Congress in 1983 claims that federal agents are not enforcing rules that are supposed to protect some of those who participate in medical research. This laxness "could . . . [expose] patients to unnecessary risks," the report concludes.

Research Subjects and Informed Consent

A second reason ethical rules for human experimentation are difficult to follow has to do with informed consent. We've already seen some of the considerations that complicate that issue in ordinary day-to-day medicine. When it comes to research, the complications proliferate.

Suppose, for example, a doctor gets a group of patients to take an experimental new drug. The doctor's job is to monitor the patients and see how many show signs of improved health.

Chances are a good percentage will, at least at first. The patients could be so encouraged by the idea of getting a new medicine that they feel better. They might enjoy the contact with the researcher and feel better because of that, or they could just feel good at being part of a worthwhile project. There could be many reasons for their improvement, all of them psychological. The reasons might have nothing to do with the new medicine itself.

That is why scientists need a control group for certain tests. Volunteers in the control group are told that they will receive a new drug or undergo a new procedure, but they do not. Instead, they get a placebo, a harmless substance (or procedure) that looks, feels, smells, tastes, or is administered exactly like the genuine treatment. This allows researchers to separate psychological from actual effects. People in both groups may think they feel better during an experiment. But only if those who are getting the real treatment show a measurable improvement can that treatment be called effective.

That is fine, as far as research goes. But what about the people in the control group? Was it moral to lie to them?

One way doctors get around this dilemma is to inform people in both groups that they may or may not genuinely receive treatment. Thus, volunteers go into the experiment knowing that they have only a chance of getting care that could help them.

However, the problem doesn't end there. In some tests, neither doctor nor patient knows who is getting treatment and who the placebo. Such double-blind tests require doctors to prescribe without knowing whether a particular patient will benefit.

The doctor's plight can be even more perplexing. He or she may have to give treatments that are almost certainly not useful, just to complete an experiment. On other occasions an experiment may require the doctor to withhold treatment that might save a life. What should physicians do when their ethical duty as HCPs collides with their ethical duty as scientists?

A third set of difficulties revolves around the question, Who can ethically be asked to act as a "human guinea pig"? In the 1980s, agreement is general that it is unethical to experiment upon humans who are unable to speak for themselves or protect themselves against possible abuses.

Should such agreement exist? A quarter of a century ago, scientists were testing experimental polio vaccines on children. A vaccine was desperately needed to protect children against the crippling, often fatal disease. But no one knew whether the experimental vaccines would work. "When you innoculate children with a polio vaccine," said Dr. Jonas Salk, who developed one of the vaccines, "you don't sleep well for two or three months." Would Dr. Salk's experiments be considered ethical according to today's standards? The National Commission for the Protection of Human Subjects says that experiments on children cannot be justified unless the risk to each child is minimal. Only if a risky experiment holds the promise of direct benefit to a child is it permissible. The polio experiments were risky, and many who participated in them might never have been exposed to the disease anyway. Yet, partly because of them, polio has been virtually eliminated.

Upon Whom May Researchers Experiment?

What about others who cannot speak on their own behalf? Some scientists argue that people who have sunk into deep comas are ideal for testing certain drugs on, or that student doctors should be allowed to practice their skills on the unconscious. There are those who believe that the mentally ill or retarded should be made available for research. Many contend that research cries out to be done on pregnant women and nursing mothers. How else can doctors determine what drugs or foods may be dangerous to the health of fetuses or breast-fed infants? Fetuses themselves—aborted ones—are a useful source of human tissue for experimental purposes. But is using fetuses for research ethical?

The National Commission, in separate reports, has issued guidelines to cover some of these groups. It approved research on pregnant women, research that might result in harm to their unborn infants, provided those women were already scheduled to undergo abortions later. It recommended that research on pregnant women be subject to informed consent. (In some cases, the father as well as the mother of the unborn child must give consent.) As far as the mentally incompetent are concerned, the commission's guidelines are even more stringent than those it drew up for children.

Who else is available for needed medical research? The sick certainly are, but we have seen some of the ethical problems that limit their use for this purpose. Healthy men and women are a possibility as well. Such volunteers may be students, especially medical students. Students appear to be excellent for the purpose. Most are young and reasonably discerning. Most are equipped to judge an experiment's worth and to decide how its risks and benefits measure up for them. Yet even here, troublesome questions arise. The most enlightened of students can be maneuvered into doing something that they do not really want to do. Professors can hint that good grades await those who volunteer for the experiments they are conducting. Sometimes students are paid for participating in research projects. Although the pay is generally low, it could persuade needy students to volunteer for experiments that they may not feel entirely comfortable about.

Prisoners furnish another traditional pool of research volunteers. Early English experiments with smallpox vaccines were conducted on men in jail. Among the volunteers for further artificial heart implants have been several of the hundreds of men waiting on death rows around the United States.

The objection that some make to using students as research subjects also applies to using prisoners. Can it be that prisoners volunteer because they have been promised or think they have been promised that doing so will help them win parole? Another consideration recalls one of the objections to using medicine as a tool of punishment. Can an incarcerated person ever make a choice that is truly free? Isn't there always some element of coercion about it? Believing there must be, the National Commission recommended against allowing prisoners to offer themselves for experiments.

What does it all mean? Some scientists fear that overconcern for bioethical niceties may soon make it impossible to find suitable human research subjects in the United States. Others take a different view. The concern simply means, they say, that from now on, experimenters will be as solicitous about their human subjects as they are about their own work and their own ambitions. It means there will be no more experiments as corrupt as those performed in Tuskegee or at Willowbrook or the Jewish Chronic Disease Hospital. It means protection for every potential human subject.

In our fast-paced medical world, that protection could be vital. An American today can become the subject of an experiment without being helpless or poor or a member of a minority or mentally infirm. Barney Clark and William Schroeder weren't any of these. They were just men who happened to be seriously ill.

And that is what makes it unlikely that the pool of human research subjects will dry up. Almost anyone could be in a position like Dr. Clark's or William Schroeder's someday. Any accident victim or anyone with a major illness could be offered a chance to undergo an experimental procedure. In the 1980s, the line between therapeutic medicine—medicine intended to relieve suffering or to cure—and experimental medicine has become very thin indeed. It is a line that any of us could be asked to cross someday. And if we are asked to cross that line, we want to know that we will be protected on the other side.

6

At the Brink of Life

The birth of any set of quadruplets is unusual, but the four boys born to an Australian couple, Graham and Helen Muir, in January 1984, were even more unusual than most. The babies were not conceived inside their mother's body, for in ten years of marriage Helen Muir had not been able to become pregnant. Instead, doctors had surgically removed some of Mrs. Muir's reproductive egg cells. They fertilized four of the eggs with sperm from her husband. This fertilization took place in a small laboratory vessel called a petri dish. Because a petri dish is made of glass, the procedure is formally known as in vitro (in glass) fertilization. Next, the doctors placed the zygotes, the fertilized eggs, back in Mrs. Muir's body. Nine months later, the "test-tube" quads were born.

For another childless couple, the path to parenthood was different. Although this husband and wife had recently moved from an unsatisfactory home into a lovely new neighborhood, their lack of a family continued to sadden them. Eventually, the wife offered to choose another woman to bear her husband's child. Then, she said, she and her husband could raise that child as their own. The husband agreed, and a surrogate (substitute) mother—a young domestic worker from a foreign country—was selected.

Tragedy struck a third couple while they were young. Just after his twenty-third birthday, the husband learned he was fatally ill. His wife wanted his baby, but not then, not while he was dying and she was so unhappy. Her solution: artificial insemination. Some of her husband's sperm would be stored in a "sperm bank." There it would remain after his death. When she felt able to, the wife would go to a doctor's office to be inseminated with it. Her child and her husband's would be born after all.

For another young wife, pregnancy had come easily and often. Already the mother of four, she was pregnant again. After this one was born, she decided she would start taking birth-control pills.

A second pregnant woman—young and unmarried—felt she faced disaster. The father of her child-to-be had flatly refused to marry her. Briefly, she considered having the child and giving it up for adoption, but in the end, she did not feel she could bear to do so. Abortion, she concluded, was the only answer.

Five stories, all different, but all with one thing in common. Each involves human intervention in the human reproductive process. Each is an example of human beings deciding whether or not other human beings will be born.

To Intervene or Not to Intervene

Is it ethical for humans to make such decisions? Some have no doubt that it is. Every woman has the absolute right to do whatever she wants with her own body, they say. No one should force a woman to run the risk of becoming pregnant if she does not wish to, or to bear a child she does not want. By the same token, childless women have every right to avail themselves of any medical technology that may help them have a family.

Others are equally firm in their belief that it is wrong for humans ever to intervene in the creation of life. That is a matter for God alone, they maintain. It is unethical to use medicine in any way to help create or destroy a new life.

Between these two extremes is a wide range of opinion.
Into it fall the attitudes of a majority of Americans, HCPs
and laypeople alike. To them, the question of human intervention
in the reproductive process is not a simple choice between certain
good and utter evil. Some intervention, they assume, is necessary
and desirable. Yet intervention cannot be justified in every
instance. The dilemma lies in deciding which cases call for
intervention and which do not.

After all, intervention goes on all the time. Slapping a newborn
on the bottom to make it start crying—and breathing—is an old-
fashioned intervention aimed at saving a life. More up-to-date
interventions include putting a premature infant in an incubator
or on a respirator. Ordering a woman with a difficult pregnancy
to stay in bed for weeks at a time to avoid a miscarriage is an
intervention, too. Such interventions are so commonplace that
we may not think of them as interventions at all. But they are.

Intervention isn't new, either. Egyptian women relied
on birth control to prevent pregnancies in the time of the
Pharaohs. Birth control was used in Ancient Greece and Rome,
and abortions were frequent in both places as well. The first
deliberate insemination of a woman by artificial means occurred
in London in 1785. In vitro fertilization is new—its successful
use in humans goes back only to 1978—but surrogate motherhood
is not. The husband and wife mentioned earlier who found a
surrogate to give them a child did so over 4,000 years ago. Their
names were Abraham and Sarah, and the surrogate was Hagar,
Sarah's Egyptian maid. Their story is told in the Bible.

For Sarah and Abraham, using a surrogate in order to
become parents was relatively straightforward. For people
involved in surrogate motherhood today, however, the process
is more complex.

Surrogate Motherhood

In 1982, a man named Alexander Malahoff signed a contract
with a young married woman who agreed to act as a surrogate
mother. The woman, Judy Stiver, was artificially inseminated,
and Malahoff promised to pay her $10,000 when his baby was
born. That baby, he hoped, would be what he needed to convince
his own estranged wife to return and resume their marriage.

The baby—a boy—was born early the next year. Delighted, Malahoff had him baptized.

Trouble soon began. It turned out that the infant was mentally retarded. Suddenly, Malahoff no longer wanted the boy. In fact, he charged, Judy Stiver had cheated him. Not he, but someone else, was the real father.

Where did this leave the baby? Severely handicapped and likely to require special care throughout his life, he had no one to give him that care. Malahoff had rejected him. The Stivers said they would not be responsible.

The end of the story is not particularly happy. Blood tests proved Malahoff right; he was not the father. Faced with this evidence, the Stivers gave in and agreed to keep the child.

With all its ethical complications, surrogate motherhood is becoming more common in the United States. In 1983, a center for bringing together potential surrogates and infertile wives opened in New York City. Within four months, fifteen couples had signed up for its services.

Couples who inquire about using the center are warned that they can expect to pay up to $25,000 before getting a baby. Of that, about $8,000 goes to the center and $10,000 to the surrogate. The rest is spent in legal fees. In New York, as elsewhere around the country, surrogate motherhood is legal, although state adoption and legitimacy laws complicate it. Michigan law, for instance, allows surrogates to bear children, but forbids their receiving payment. Children born to surrogates in that state are considered illegitimate. At least twelve states are considering legislation to regulate—or ban—the use of surrogate mothers. Such laws, their sponsors say, would protect children like Judy Stiver's baby. As it is now, "the child is simply left in limbo," according to one New York lawmaker.

Things were simpler in Old Testament times. Abraham did not doubt that Ishmael was his son, but even if he had, there existed no sophisticated blood test to prove him right. Ishmael was not retarded, but had he been, his condition probably would not have been diagnosed at birth. So although surrogate motherhood is far from new, it has, like other bioethical issues, been given a new twist by the advances of modern medicine. The same is true of other forms of human intervention in reproduction.

Of all those forms of intervention, none is more highly charged emotionally than abortion. And as we will see, the abortion issue is a major factor in the bioethical debate over other reproductive interventions as well.

Abortion, Past and Present

The idea that abortion is immoral is rather new. Even though the Hippocratic oath forbade doctors to perform abortions, it is unlikely that Hippocrates considered the procedure wrong in itself. In the Greece of his day, abortion, as well as infanticide and abandonment of unwanted babies, was widely accepted. Hippocrates included other prohibitions in his oath; for instance, he required physicians to promise not to "use the knife," but to leave that kind of work to surgeons. Presumably, he thought people other than doctors should perform abortions too.

For hundreds of years, abortion continued to be openly practiced. In Europe, it was often used as a kind of after-the-fact birth control, especially during the first trimester (the first three months of pregnancy). Then, in 1869, for the first time, the Roman Catholic Church condemned the procedure. Within a short time, abortion was made a crime in many countries, including the United States.

So abortion moved around to back streets and dingy alleys. Despairing girls and women who felt they could not go through with a pregnancy found themselves being operated upon—and sometimes dying—in filthy cellars and attics. Abortionists were frequently incompetent, their instruments unclean, and their procedures brutal, yet they charged exorbitant rates. Such conditions kept many pregnant women from seeking an abortion, and thousands gave birth to children they did not want and had little means of caring for. Only those who were lucky enough to locate a safe abortionist or rich enough to travel to a place where abortion was legal had the opportunity to end their pregnancies without serious danger.

That was the situation in forty-six of the fifty states until 1973. Then, on January 22 of that year, the United States Supreme Court overturned state laws that prohibited abortions during the first two trimesters of pregnancy. The court based its ruling upon the privacy issue. Under the United States

Constitution, it said, every woman has the right to make her own personal medical decisions in private, after consulting with her doctor. Cities and states cannot pass or enforce laws meant to come between doctor and patient.

Now that abortion was legal, women began availing themselves of it. By 1983, abortions were numbering 1.6 million a year. That meant that one-third of all American pregnancies were ending in abortion. It did not mean, however, that the abortion issue was settled.

"Pro-Choice" and "Pro-Life"

While abortion was illegal, the fight to change abortion laws was waged by those who believed in women's moral right to choose whether or not to bear a child. Such people refer to themselves as being "pro-choice." Since the Supreme Court's 1973 decision, it has been anti-abortionists—members of "pro-life" groups—who have sought to alter the law. Of the many anti-abortion committees working in this country today, the best known is the Right-to-Life organization.

Right-to-Life's goal is to amend—change—the Constitution to outlaw abortion once more. The group's proposed amendment states that from the very moment of conception there exists a full human being with all the rights and privileges of any other American citizen.

Does human life exist from conception? Certainly, from the instant an egg is fertilized a process begins that can, if all goes well, lead to the development of a multicelled blastula that will grow into an embryo and then into a fetus. The process will end in the birth of a human child.

But is the potential to become a human being the same thing as being a legal citizen? No, it is not, say those who advocate a woman's right to choose abortion. Never before has anyone suggested that a zygote has legal status. Right-to-Lifers say it today only to bolster their anti-abortion argument, pro-choicers add. The Supreme Court agrees. "There has always been strong support for the view that life does not begin until live birth," wrote Justice Harry Blackmun in the court's 1973 decision.

Right-to-Life hopes to change that through its proposed amendment. Until and unless that amendment becomes part of the Constitution, though, or the Supreme Court changes its mind, abortion will remain legal in the United States. That means we will have to contend with a growing number of ever-more-difficult questions relating to it, and to other forms of reproductive intervention.

A Matter of Timing

One question is when. At what point during a pregnancy may abortions be performed? According to the Supreme Court's 1973 decision, a woman may undergo the procedure at any time before the fetus is viable—that is, before it can survive on its own outside the mother's body. In 1973, that meant a fetus could be aborted if the woman was as much as twenty-seven weeks pregnant. At that point a fetus weighs about 2.5 pounds. Ten or fifteen years ago, such a tiny baby had small chance of surviving.

But medical technology has changed, and a fetus that was not viable in 1973 may well survive today. In 1984, the survival rate for 2.5-pound babies was close to 100 percent. Can HCPs ethically abort fetuses of that size? "The area of late abortions is one of our most difficult areas," comments an obstetrician at Columbia-Presbyterian Medical Center in New York City. "There are no easy answers, given our technology now." In an effort to provide some kind of answer, New York state has outlawed abortions after the twenty-fourth week. Some hospitals limit them further, not permitting them after the twentieth week.

But what if, even with such limits, an abortion results in a live birth? This is an exceedingly rare occurrence, but it has happened. In 1982, New York City health records showed eighteen live births out of 160,000 abortions.

Should live-born fetuses scheduled for abortion be left to die? Or should doctors do all they can to try to save them? Who should decide? Who will be responsible for such infants if they do live? Who will pay their medical bills?

As of 1984, such questions were mostly being answered on a hospital-by-hospital basis. Only in California had lawmakers attempted to deal with the problem. Under that state's law,

"The rights to medical treatment of an infant prematurely born alive in the course of an abortion shall be the same as the rights of an infant of similar medical status prematurely born spontaneously."

On the surface, that sounds wise and humane, but how will the law work out in practice? "If a fetus survives an abortion there will be every reason to fear that it has been severely damaged by the procedure," wrote Harvard University ethicist Sissela Bok. "As a result, any law requiring the maintenance of life in such survivors might result in extraordinary suffering on the part of those who are rescued." More simply, Dr. Bok is saying that life could be worse than death for live-born aborted infants.

Dr. William Caspe, director of pediatrics at Bronx-Lebanon Hospital in New York, shares her concern. "What are the chances of a twenty-four-week fetus to have a normal life?" he asks. "Probably small." The likelihood that such an infant will be physically and mentally handicapped is overwhelming.

Can the dilemma be avoided by passing laws to limit abortions to the first trimester? In many cases, such limits would be perfectly workable. Already, most abortions do take place within the first three months. The United States Centers for Disease Control in Atlanta, Georgia, estimates that over 90 percent of all abortions occur before the twelfth week of pregnancy. Another 9 percent are scheduled before the twentieth week. Less than 1 percent, only 13,000 abortions a year, come after the twenty-first week, and it is only among them that a live birth could presently occur.

Eliminating all abortions after the twenty-first week, however, may not be possible. In some cases, a woman or her doctor may have miscalculated the state of her pregnancy. A woman who thinks she is only seventeen or eighteen weeks pregnant may actually be twenty or twenty-one weeks along. In other cases, a woman may not even have been considering abortion; then, well into her second trimester, she recognizes a problem. Yet once she has considered it, she may decide she has every reason for going ahead with it. That's because of a new diagnostic technique called amniocentesis.

New Technologies, New Dilemmas

In amniocentesis, a hollow needle is inserted through a pregnant woman's abdomen and into the amniotic fluid that surrounds the fetus. Some of the fluid is drawn off through the needle. Analyzed in a laboratory, this fluid can tell doctors much about the child that is to be born.

It can tell them the child's sex and what its coloring will be. More important, amniocentesis shows when a fetus has a strong chance of being born with certain abnormalities. The test reveals the presence of Down's syndrome, for example. Down's produces mental retardation. Amniocentesis can pick up other conditions, too, such as Tay-Sachs disease. Tay-Sachs children appear normal at birth, but within six months symptoms—blindness, paralysis, dementia, retardation—show up. Victims of this disease invariably die, usually before their fourth birthdays.

Useful a diagnostic tool as amniocentesis is, it badly complicates the late-abortion issue. The procedure cannot be performed until the fourteenth to the seventeenth week of pregnancy. Results may not be available until the twenty-first week. By then, the fetus could be viable.

This disadvantage of amniocentesis could be corrected by a still newer procedure used for detecting fetal abnormalities. The procedure is called chorionic biopsy. In it, a small piece of the placenta is removed and analyzed. The placenta is the membrane through which food, oxygen, and wastes are exchanged between mother and fetus. The procedure can be done as early as the seventh week of pregnancy. Preliminary results are known within four to six hours.

In terms of time, of scheduling an abortion as early as possible, chorionic biopsy represents an improvement over amniocentesis. However, in the mid-1980s the new technique was still in the testing stages. It was available to very few women, since chorionic biopsies were being performed at only four hospitals around the nation. Furthermore, chorionic biopsy appears to result in a large number of miscarriages. Up to 10 percent of women who undergo it may lose their babies. Most important of all, chorionic biopsy resolves only one of the ethical problems involved in screening for fetal defects—the problem of timing. Other complications remain.

One involves deciding which fetal abnormalities call for abortion and which do not. Many people might agree that the parents of a Tay-Sachs fetus have good reason to choose abortion. But what about the parents of a child with Down's syndrome? Some Down's children are profoundly retarded; others moderately so. Some victims of the condition are physically handicapped, but others are not. Some may have to be institutionalized for life. Others can help to support themselves by working at routine jobs in a sheltered environment. They may be able to lead semi-independent lives in group homes. Is it right to deny life to someone capable of that much? On the other hand, parents can't know ahead of time precisely how badly handicapped their child may turn out to be. Don't they have the right to use medical technology to help them produce the healthiest possible child?

But what if parents begin using techniques like amniocentesis and chorionic biopsy to produce not just the healthiest child but the one they consider the most perfect in every way? Parents eager for a blue-eyed son may decide to abort any brown-eyed daughter the wife happens to be carrying. Parents of twins may ask a doctor to abort the one that seems smaller and weaker. How would society react if fetal analysis becomes a tool to fashion "designer children"?

Added to these considerations is the fact that this analysis must be examined in relation to other reproductive interventions. What if an abnormality is apparent in a child conceived in vitro or by artificial insemination? What about a child carried by a surrogate mother? Could the biological father force her to have an abortion?

Such questions will be asked more and more frequently in the months and years ahead. By combining amniocentesis or chorionic biopsy with blood tests and ultrasound screening— the use of sound waves to form computerized images of the fetus—doctors can already isolate nearly two hundred separate fetal disorders. More will undoubtedly become detectable before long. Any one of them could be seen as grounds for abortion.

For this reason, some people believe that amniocentesis and other fetal screening methods should not be used.

Modern medical technology has created problems and questions like the ones we've been examining in this chapter. Can modern medicine also solve the problems and answer the questions?

Surgery Before Birth?

The story "Surgical Miracles Inside the Womb" appeared in a 1983 issue of *Life* magazine. It did ring of the miraculous. Doctors had discovered that a fetus was hydrocephalic. Fluid building up around his brain made it likely that the boy would be born blind and retarded.

So doctors operated on the unborn child. When his mother was five months pregnant, they inserted into his skull a tube that allowed them to drain off the excess fluid. The child was born, and at age two, seemed perfectly normal. Other fetuses have been treated experimentally, both surgically and with drugs, while in utero, inside the womb.

Will in utero treatment one day replace second trimester abortion as a means of producing healthy infants? John C. Fletcher, a bioethicist at the National Institutes of Health in Bethesda, Maryland, is cautious. Records kept by the International Fetal Surgical Registry in Manitoba, Canada, show that of twenty-five fetuses treated for hydrocephalus, twenty-one survived. Of those, twelve—more than half—are moderately or severely handicapped. Of thirty-five fetuses treated for urinary-tract disorders, twenty-one died.

Dr. Fletcher points to other ethical problems. What if a pregnant woman whose child is deemed to need fetal surgery refuses to undergo it? Surely she has every right to do so. The surgery, after all, will be performed in her body, and as New York Supreme Court Justice Benjamin Cardozo said nearly three-quarters of a century ago, "Every human being . . . has a right to determine what should be done with his own body."

Besides, what would the ramifications be if women start being forced to undergo treatment whose aim is to help, not them, but someone else? Would that mean others will similarly be compelled to sacrifice themselves for another's health? The answer could be yes. "A society willing to coerce a woman into surgery for a . . . fetus must surely be willing to coerce a father to sacrifice a kidney for his child," Fletcher warns.

Dr. Fletcher is not the only one with bioethical concerns. In 1982 and 1983, doctors and other HCPs met to discuss fetal surgery and to try to devise some guidelines for its use. One point upon which most agreed was that if such surgery is to be done, it must be performed in a way that presents the least possible risk to both fetus and mother. The doctors were critical of some past fetal surgery that, in their opinion, placed patients at needless risk. The doctors also agreed that plans for any such surgery should be reviewed by an ethics committee similar to the Institutional Review Boards needed to approve human experimentation. The physicians added that these committees should include laypeople to shield patients from doctors who are overeager to test new techniques.

Bioethicists are encouraged by the doctors' caution and by their unwillingness to rush into fetal surgery before debating some of its ethical implications. Still, the caution and the discouraging statistics on in utero surgery suggest that the technique will not quickly replace late abortion as a means of dealing with fetal abnormalities. The bioethical problems raised by procedures like amniocentesis and chorionic biopsy will continue to be debated and discussed.

Other Issues, Other Problems

Debate will continue over other reproductive issues, as well. And those debates will become more complex as medical science advances and as we decide how our society can best take advantage of those advances in reproductive medicine. For example:

- Should all pregnant women be given the opportunity to undergo amniocentesis? Be required to undergo it? Some argue that requiring it would benefit society by reducing the size of our handicapped population. But even if that were a worthwhile goal (and many would say it is not), how would doctors go about achieving it? By forcing unwilling women to abort fetuses judged abnormal? Who would judge? On what basis would the judgments be made?

- Can fetuses be used for research? As we saw in Chapter 5, the National Commission for the Protection of Human Subjects has approved such research, provided the fetus was due to be aborted anyway. But what if a woman were to become pregnant with the express intention of producing a research fetus? What if some offered fetuses for sale? If someone were to set up a business of buying and selling them?

- Can fetuses be "organ farms"? In a scenario suggested by the Hastings Center, the New York institute that studies bioethical issues, the wife of a man who is dying of kidney disease offers to become pregnant and have an abortion at six months. The kidneys from the fetus will then be transplanted into her husband's body. Would this be ethical? the Center asks.

- Is in vitro fertilization a form of abortion? Recent findings show that the technique works best if more than one egg is used. Consequently, doctors at this country's forty-six in vitro clinics give patients large doses of female hormones to stimulate their bodies to produce more eggs. But many of the eggs are destroyed after fertilization. Is it moral to allow that to happen? Because of such considerations, the United States Congress banned in vitro research in 1974. The ban was lifted the next year, but no money has been appropriated for new research. However, clinical applications of the technique go on, and over two hundred test-tube babies have been born worldwide.

- Do some forms of birth control amount to abortion? Although the Catholic Church officially forbids it, the use of birth control is widespread in the United States, even among Catholic couples. The traditional methods of simply putting a physical barrier between egg and sperm or taking pills to disrupt the production of eggs seem acceptable to most Americans. But the "morning-after" pill, now growing in popularity, is different. It destroys an egg that has already been fertilized.

Could we avoid most of the bioethical questions we have looked at in this chapter simply by putting an end to research into new means to help create life; by forbidding the use of such techniques as amniocentesis; by adopting the Right-to-Life amendment? In a sense, we could. If we do take such steps, we will be calling a halt to an era of growing human intervention in the reproductive process. In vitro clinics will shut down. Doctors will stop performing artificial inseminations and prescribing certain forms of birth control. Girls and women will no longer be able to get legal abortions. Parents will not have to agonize over whether to abort a Down's syndrome child or one with Tay-Sachs disease.

But if outlawing reproductive intervention would eliminate some bioethical problems, it would create others. Men and women unable to become parents without medical help will once more be condemned to childlessness. Is it ethical to take away their chance to have families? Physicians, fully aware of their ability to diagnose many fetal disorders, will have to allow the birth of infants doomed to lifetimes of illness or to early, miserable deaths. Is it ethical to prevent doctors from relieving suffering when it is within their power to do so? Abortion will return to the back streets, and the young, the poor, and the powerless will follow it there, while the richer and more sophisticated find their way to reliable abortionists elsewhere. Is it right for safe medicine to be available to the rich but not to the poor?

The medical knowledge gained in recent decades is here to stay. Neither it nor the bioethical problems it helps create can be wished away. The technology and the problems can only be confronted and debated.

7

Genetic Engineering

Among the most devastating of human illnesses is a condition known as Huntington's disease. Huntington's usually strikes its victims when they are between the ages of thirty and fifty. At first it may not seem to be a disease at all, just simple bad temper. Irritability and moodiness are two of its earliest signs. Then come more definite symptoms. The face, neck, and arms move jerkily. Twitching muscles in lips and tongue begin to make talking difficult. Before long, this motor impairment spreads. People with Huntington's walk with a shuffling gait. Mood swings become more violent. Some victims commit suicide; others have to be placed in mental hospitals. Intellectual activity deteriorates too, with loss of attention span and memory failure. There is no known treatment for the disease, and death generally occurs within fifteen years of its onset.

Fortunately, Huntington's is rare. For a few people, though, the likelihood of getting it is high. That is because Huntington's runs in families. The children of diseased individuals have a 50 percent chance of getting it. For this reason, doctors have tended to discourage men and women with a family history of the illness from becoming parents.

Yet that is not always possible. Not everyone is aware of his or her family medical history. What is more, since Huntington's may not show up until middle age, people may not discover that they have it until after they have had children—even grandchildren.

That is why the news that came out of Boston's Massachusetts General Hospital in 1983 was so welcome. Late that year, a research team led by Dr. James Gusella announced that it might be on the way to finding a method of diagnosing Huntington's early.

Dr. Gusella and his coworkers broke apart samples of cell material from people suffering from Huntington's. On one specific part of that material, they found an abnormality, or a marker, that they believe indicates the presence of the disease. If their theory is correct, many of those who have Huntington's and who may transmit it to their offspring carry a similar marker. By testing for the marker, doctors may one day be able to determine precisely which members of a Huntington's family have the disease and which do not.

The new knowledge could do more than provide a means of diagnosing Huntington's before its symptoms appear. Further investigation may tell scientists how the condition develops. Knowing that might enable them to create effective treatments. Eventually, scientists may even learn to correct the biological defect that leads to Huntington's. If that happens, it will be a great triumph for genetic engineering.

Genetic engineering is a new science—and a controversial one. It involves the manipulation and alteration of inborn characteristics—such as the inherited factor that leads to the development of Huntington's disease. This manipulation and alteration is done by human beings. And that is where the controversy comes in.

To some people, genetic engineering appears to be a marvelous—almost a miraculous—new tool for fighting and conquering disease. "We celebrate the healing possibilities that are now before us through this new life-technology," said a document issued in November 1982 by the National Council of Churches of Christ. The optimism was echoed by the President's Commission for the Study of Ethical Problems in Medicine and Biomedical and Behavioral Research. In 1982, commission members released their report on genetic engineering.

According to that report, further research into genetic engineering appears to be desirable—even a "duty." A duty to whom? Not merely to the relatively small number of men and women who live with the threat of developing Huntington's. Using the procedure pioneered by Dr. Gusella, scientists may someday be able to diagnose up to 3,000 other inherited diseases. Today, no one even knows what causes these diseases. One promise of genetic engineering is that it offers the potential of wiping them out altogether.

But some people have an entirely different view of genetic engineering and of what it promises for the future. To them the new technology seems both dangerous and immoral. They see it as the ultimate—and ultimately unethical—human intervention into nature—or the work of God.

Genes and Genetic Inheritance

Genes are the basic units of inheritance. They are what make a plant or animal—or a human being—resemble its parents. They allow that plant, animal, or person to pass its own characteristics along to *its* offspring. So far, scientists have been able to distinguish about 50,000 separate human genes.

Working in groups, these genes make each person the individual he or she is. One group of genes gives Rebecca her blond hair. Another group is responsible for the wave in that hair. Still another gives her a row of light freckles across the bridge of her nose, and so on.

How do genes do this? To answer that question, let's take a closer look at what genes are.

Genes are parts of deoxyribonucleic acid—DNA, for short. For all living things, DNA is the carrier of genetic information. Inside each of your body cells is a tightly coiled microscopic thread of DNA. If that thread were uncoiled, it would be longer than you are tall.

Greatly magnified, the DNA molecule looks like a spiral ladder. The DNA molecule in one of your cells is a "ladder" made up of some 10 billion rungs. Chemically coded into those rungs is the genetic "message" that makes you what you are.

Half of that DNA message came from your mother, half from your father.

It has been said that if all the information contained in one human DNA molecule could be put into English, it would fill a thousand-volume encyclopedia—with about a thousand pages to each volume. Each gene is a small part of this enormous message.

Genes usually reproduce their part of the message exactly. Freckles and light wavy hair run in Rebecca's family. Rebecca will pass the genes that produce these features on to her own children and grandchildren. Depending upon the genetic traits these children and grandchildren inherit from other members of their families, they will resemble Rebecca to a greater or lesser degree.

Sometimes, though, genes do not reproduce their messages precisely. Tiny changes—mutations—may occur. Such mutations may affect any aspect of a person's genetic structure. Once a mutation does occur, chances are it will be passed along to succeeding generations. Remember, genes *usually* reproduce their messages faithfully.

Some mutations produce serious abnormalities. One gene mutation might cause a person to have red blood cells that are misshapen. If the cells are sufficiently deformed, the person may not be able to absorb enough oxygen. Another mutation might mean that a person's body is unable to manufacture a certain substance needed for normal growth. When a serious abnormality of this kind appears, we say that the affected individual has a genetic disease.

Genetic Diseases

Scientists have isolated about 3,000 human genetic diseases. Some are mild, but many are not. Tay-Sachs disease, mentioned in Chapter 6, is a genetic disease. It is found only among Jewish people from Eastern Europe and their descendants. A serious genetic disease that attacks some people of African descent is sickle-cell anemia. Other genetic diseases include Down's syndrome, albinism (in which a person lacks normal coloring in eyes, hair, and skin), and hemophilia, sometimes called bleeders' disease.

Genetic diseases are relatively rare. That is because, in many cases, both parents must carry the gene for a particular disease in order to pass it on to a child. If both parents do carry the abnormal gene, the chance of their children having the disease becomes substantial. It is for this reason that couples who know they may be carriers often turn to amniocentesis or chorionic biopsy. Such procedures can usually tell them if a fetus is affected well before the expected time of delivery. If it is affected, the parents must decide whether or not to seek an abortion.

But what if they didn't have to make that decision? What if doctors were able to correct the defective gene so that the child could be born healthy? Finding ways to treat genetic disease is one of the medical goals of genetic engineering. It is among the "healing possibilities" that the National Council of Churches of Christ was applauding in November 1982.

Genetic Engineering—What Does It Involve?

Before that possibility can become reality, scientists must learn precisely how to turn defective genes into perfect ones. One of their experiments involves a two-step process. First, they would combine parts of normal genes—bits of DNA—in a test tube. Then they would introduce this recombinant DNA into the diseased person's genetic structure. The recombinant DNA would take the place of the abnormal gene. With the defective gene no longer present, the disease could not be transmitted.

Not only is a process like this possible in theory, it has been accomplished in the laboratory. Scientists have already been able to change the genetic structure of such simple life forms as bacteria.

One kind of man-made bacteria has been constructed by a team of scientists in California. These bacteria appear to have the ability to prevent frost from forming on potato plants. By 1983, the California scientists were prepared to begin testing their bacteria on potato crops in the state.

Other scientists have attempted genetic engineering in animals. In one experiment, they inserted into mouse zygotes a gene that controls growth in rats. Result: "supermice" that grew bigger and more rapidly than ordinary mice.

Gene therapy has even been tried experimentally in human subjects. In the late 1970s, two patients with a genetic blood disease called thalassemia agreed to allow scientists to try to correct their conditions through genetic engineering. The scientists tried to cure the patients by transplanting healthy genes into their bone marrow, but they failed.

The thalassemia experiment excited a great deal of controversy. A number of scientists criticized the experimenters for going ahead with gene therapy before they knew enough to give the procedure a real chance of success. In the 1970s, scientists did not have enough basic knowledge about genetics to attempt such a bold experiment, the critics said. For the promise of genetic engineering as a tool of medicine is matched only by the threat it could pose to human society and civilization.

The Ethics of Genetic Engineering

The first problem is that which attends any new medical experimentation, the threat to the research subjects themselves. Only a small percentage of the mouse zygotes treated with genetic material from rats developed into supermice, for instance. Most failed to survive. The odds of survival for human subjects will have to be better than they were for the mice. The National Institutes of Health (NIH) will not give permission for genetic engineering research on human beings unless the subjects are reasonably likely to benefit from the experiments. As we saw in Chapter 5, benefit to the individual patient is supposed to come first, before the scientific search for pure knowledge.

A second problem is more complex, since it involves the very nature of genetic structure. Suppose the transplanted material affects not the defective gene it was intended to repair but other nearby genes. A mutation could occur. This mutation might be slight, but even a small genetic change can be devastating to an organism. In seeking to correct Tay-Sachs disease in a fetus, for example, doctors might produce an infant with an equally terrible condition. The supermice experiments confirm that slipups can occur. In two cases, strange mutations proved fatal to the little creatures.

There are other more far-reaching threats. Imagine that scientists who are attempting to engineer a genetic change bring about a mutation that damages but does not destroy the organism. That mutation might affect its reproductive mechanism. If it does, the unwanted mutation may be passed along to succeeding generations.

The possibility of such "germline cell" mutations is real. If any do occur, they could show up in generation after generation after generation—forever. A new man-made strain of bacteria may perpetuate itself on earth. A new kind of insect or rodent might do the same. Or genetic engineers might produce a germline mutation in human beings. Then they will have brought about a permanent alteration in the human gene pool.

Carried to an extreme, this possibility suggests a scenario that sounds like something out of science fiction. Scientists accidentally create a test-tube "monster." That monster reproduces itself, and its offspring reproduce too, in ever-increasing numbers. Perhaps the new life forms overrun the earth. Perhaps they are dangerous to plant or animal life. Perhaps they threaten human beings. Perhaps they are deadly. Perhaps . . .

One who is determined to see to it that no such "perhapses" ever come to pass is a man named Jeremy Rifkin. Rifkin is an environmental activist and head of a Washington, D.C., organization called the Foundation on Economic Trends. In 1982, he drew up a petition, which he circulated among American religious leaders and scientists. Later, Rifkin presented this petition to the United States Congress. It called for a federal law to ban any research into germline therapy.

Rifkin has opposed genetic engineering research in other ways. In 1983, he went to court in an attempt to prevent California scientists from testing their man-made frost-preventing bacteria on potato crops there. Who knows what environmental effects such bacteria might have? Rifkin asks. They might destroy other bacteria that potatoes need in order to grow. They might harm other plants. Then again, they might not. No one knows, but in Rifkin's view that lack of knowledge is one very good reason for not going ahead with genetic engineering. "We believe we have a sacred obligation to say no when the pursuit of a specific technological path threatens the very existence of life itself," he said.

Others disagree with Rifkin's point of view. Late in 1984, doctors and scientists at the NIH turned down his request that they impose a ban upon all research such as that involved in the supermice project. Under Rifkin's proposal, scientists would not be permitted to transfer genetic material from one species of mammal into the germline of a member of another species. In rejecting Rifkin's request, NIH officials pointed out that such research may prove vital in the fight against many human diseases, including cancer.

To Treat or Not to Treat

As a matter of fact, NIH appeared to be encouraging doctors and scientists to proceed with experimental gene therapy in human beings. By May 1985 newly revised NIH guidelines seemed likely to permit such therapy to begin within the next year or two.

Even with the new NIH guidelines in place, however, controversies remain. One concerns deciding which conditions to try to treat through genetic engineering. A disease like sickle-cell anemia might seem to be an obvious target. Victims of this debilitating disease are weak, sickly, and in pain. Sickle-cell anemia produces infections that can last for months, strokes (even in the very young), and damaged tissue.

Dr. Ola Mae Huntley is a California mother of five, three of whom are afflicted with sickle-cell anemia. She pleads with the NIH and with society to support the scientific effort to find ways to treat genetic diseases through the procedures of genetic engineering. "Until you have had intimate contact with those who have suffered or have yourself experienced the pain, strokes, seizures, and leg ulcers; the ridicule from peers, low self-esteem, desire to die, and diminishing hope for the future associated with sickle-cell anemia, do not deny me the right to decide for myself and my children whether to try the procedures," Dr. Huntley says.

But sickle-cell anemia is a disease that strikes only one specific segment of the population—black people. And some black Americans worry about what may happen if doctors and scientists begin trying to eliminate this condition among their descendants.

Blacks know that doctors may advise black couples who are sickle-cell carriers to avoid having children. Many of the doctors who counsel their patients in this way are white. Some blacks suspect that these doctors may actually want to keep blacks from having children in order to reduce the size of the black population in the United States. A few unscrupulous white doctors might go so far as to tell blacks who are not sickle-cell carriers that they *do* have the gene for the disease, these people fear. They might urge them to abort their unborn children or to seek sterilization for themselves. A man or woman who has been sterilized is no longer able to have children.

Another fear of some members of the black community is that if doctors one day begin curing sickle-cell anemia in black fetuses, they may also start introducing other genetic changes at the same time. Suppose white society decides to manipulate black genes to create a race of men and women who are strong but stupid, perfectly equipped to perform disagreeable menial tasks? Genetic engineering would have brought about a new form of domination, one that its victims would be powerless to resist.

Whether or not such fears are justified—and many people are positive that they are not—they strike a chord with some people. Nor are all those who feel its resonance black. Americans of all races and of all social and economic backgrounds have expressed concern that some doctors or scientists might use genetic engineering to achieve certain eugenic goals.

Eugenic Goals and "Playing God"

Eugenic comes from a Greek word that means well-born. The eugenic goal of genetic engineering is that every child be born strong, healthy, and well-suited to make its way in the world.

But who is to judge what "strong," "healthy," and "well-suited" mean? Theodore Roosevelt was considered weak and puny when he was born, and he was often ill as a child, but he grew up to become a soldier, rancher, and president of the United States. Kaiser Wilhelm II of Germany was born with a withered arm. He was a proud ruler and a warlike one. Napoleon Bonaparte was short and stubby—hardly the figure of a soldier. He conquered most of Europe. Would he have conquered more if a genetic engineer had made him eight inches taller? Would the Kaiser have been a stronger monarch with two normal arms? Would Teddy Roosevelt have had such a tremendous drive to succeed if he had been born "strong" and "healthy"?

There are other questions. Suppose some future father insists that his son look exactly like him. Will he be able to take his wife to a genetic engineer and demand a made-to-order infant? What would the ethical implications of that be for the unborn child? For the wife? What rights would they have?

Or suppose parents become accustomed to being able to produce the very children of their dreams. How will that affect the wonderful diversity that is such a great strength of the human race? Creating new genes could have the effect of "crowding out" old ones. "Eliminating so-called 'bad genes' will lead to a dangerous narrowing of diversity in the gene pool," Jeremy Rifkin warns. "It is very likely that in attempting to 'perfect' the human species we will succeed in engineering our own extinction." Rifkin sees genetic engineering as a "slippery slope": placing one foot on this slope—pursuing experimental gene therapy—means an inevitable slide straight to the bottom, into a world of man-made monsters.

Others echo his concern, and express further concerns of their own. Just think of Adolf Hitler and his mad obsession with the genetic superiority of the German people. Imagine what use he might have made of genetic engineering! One group of leaders of major Protestant, Jewish, and Catholic groups did just that when they composed a letter to President Jimmy Carter in 1980. "History has shown us," they wrote, "that there will always be those who believe it appropriate to 'correct' our mental and social structures by genetic means, so as to fit their vision of humanity . . . . Those who would play God will be tempted as never before."

Perhaps they will and perhaps they won't. "Most talk of 'playing God' is silly," according to J. Robert Nelson, a theologian at Boston University. Nelson helped write the report on genetic engineering issued by the National Council of Churches of Christ in 1982. He and many others, including scientists, ethicists, and members of the clergy, believe that we human beings can learn, bit by bit, to deal with the moral problems raised by the technologies of genetic engineering. Although genetic engineering may appear to be a slippery slope, it is one we can learn to negotiate safely if doctors, ethicists, lawmakers, and laypeople work together to deal with the implications of this powerful new science.

Members of the Institute on Religion in an Age of Science (IRAS) agree. For decades, IRAS has worked to promote discussion and debate between scientists and theologians. At its 1983 convention, members of the group concluded that "the conceivable dangers from future advances in genetic engineering, as applied to humans . . . would involve individual actions, which could be controlled as the possibility arose." In other words, we ought to be able to cope with each new ethical issue as it comes along.

Most members of IRAS are more optimistic about genetic engineering and its implications for human health and well-being than are Jeremy Rifkin and those who agree with his point of view. Interestingly, even some of those who endorsed Rifkin's congressional petition share the optimism. One man who signed the petition, Richard McCormick, a Jesuit priest who teaches moral theology at Georgetown University, says he is not really sure how he feels about genetic engineering. He signed, he explains, in order to help bring the issue before the public and to get a national debate started.

Ethicist John C. Fletcher of the NIH did not sign Rifkin's petition, and he strongly protests Rifkin's position. Fletcher characterizes Rifkin's attitude as one of "stridency, paranoia, and doomsaying." He believes that Rifkin's petition was irresponsible. Its wording was alarmist, Fletcher contends. It made it appear that germline therapy is about to begin in this country. Actually, Fletcher says, such therapy is only a possibility for the distant future.

It is his hope—and the hope of others like him—that when and if that future arrives we will be prepared for it.

8

Medical Care and the Courts

On April 9, 1982, a male infant was born in a hospital in Bloomington, Indiana. At once, doctors recognized that the baby was a victim of Down's syndrome. In addition, his esophagus was blocked. Without a prompt operation to correct the condition, the baby would starve to death.

As soon as their diagnosis was complete, hospital pediatricians asked the baby's parents to consent to the operation. As we know, HCPs and hospital administrators must obtain a signed consent form before going ahead with any procedure. In the case of infants—or others who are, for some reason, unable to make a decision about their own treatment—the consent must come from a parent or legal guardian. To the dismay of the Bloomington doctors, however, the baby's parents refused permission to operate.

It is not too uncommon for health professionals to be confronted with a situation like this. Disagreement with a diagnosis, a dispute over a proposed course of treatment, a rejection of care based on religious convictions—any of these could lead a parent or guardian to withhold consent. When this happens, HCPs have a choice. They can go along with the guardian's wishes. Or they can take the guardian to court and ask a judge to issue an order that will allow them to proceed with treatment.

The Bloomington doctors followed the latter course. They submitted their medical findings to a judge and asked for a court order to permit the life-saving surgery over the parents' objections.

The parents did not dispute the diagnosis. But they saw no point in operating. Doing so would only prolong the life of an infant who was not only physically abnormal but mentally retarded—perhaps hopelessly so. And they did not want to be the parents of such an infant. The baby belonged to them, the parents argued. He was theirs. Therefore, they alone had the right to decide what medical care he should—or should not—receive.

After hearing from both sides, the judge upheld the parents' right to deny treatment. The doctors and the hospital appealed that decision, and again, a court ruled in the parents' favor. On April 15, Baby Doe (as he was called to protect his and his family's privacy) died of starvation.

The Baby Doe Rule Is Born

Baby Doe's death created a storm. Many Americans were horrified by the parents' decision and shocked that the courts had refused to step in. Right-to-Life groups bitterly attacked the failure to order surgery. So did a number of organizations that promote the rights of the handicapped.

Baby Doe's death set off a political uproar too. Within days, President Ronald Reagan ordered the Department of Health and Human Services to issue a new rule to protect such babies. The regulation—immediately dubbed the Baby Doe Rule—required doctors to do everything possible to save the lives of all newborns, no matter how handicapped they might be. Even if death were certain, the federal government said, every available life-prolonging technique must be employed.

Health and Human Services administrators also notified the nation's hospitals that if they ignored the new rule, they would no longer receive any federal funding. Federal money, including that which helps pay the bills of elderly and needy patients, is an important source of income at most hospitals. Finally, agency officials ordered that the Baby Doe Rule be posted in prominent locations in every hospital. Each sign was to include a telephone number, a toll-free, twenty-four-hour-a-day hot line. Patients and visitors as well as hospital employees were urged to use this hot line to report suspected instances of neglect of handicapped newborns.

The hot line got an extensive workout. Hundreds of calls poured in, the majority of them from Right-to-Life activists, nurses doubtful about the treatment ordered by a physician, or aides who did not fully understand the type of care being given. Officials recognized most of the calls as obvious false alarms, but in a few cases, they dispatched "Baby Doe squads" to pay surprise nighttime visits to pediatric intensive-care units. In no case did a squad find any violation of law.

Outraged by the new rule and by the disruptive way it was being enforced, HCPs and hospital administrators reacted vigorously. Within weeks, the American Academy of Pediatrics (AAP) was challenging the Baby Doe Rule in court. Before a year was up, the doctors had won their case. The judge who overturned the rule called it "arbitrary" and "ill-considered." He also noted that in its haste to respond to Right-to-Life pressure, the Department of Health and Human Services had acted illegally. It had neglected to allow the sixty-day period of comment and discussion that is required before any new federal regulation goes into effect. If the department still wanted to safeguard the rights of handicapped newborns, it would have to start over.

The agency did start over, and this time it followed the rules. Officials at the department reworded the regulation slightly and invited comments. Over 17,000 flooded in. The number of comments and the variety of issues they covered indicated how deeply concerned Americans are about the ethics of choosing medical care for those who are unable to speak for themselves.

Can Caring Be Too Cruel?

One area of concern was this: How much suffering is it right to impose on an infant in an effort to save its life?

In a modern American hospital, the amount of suffering can be enormous. Writing in the July 1979 issue of the *Atlantic*, Robert and Peggy Stinson tell of the agony inflicted, against their will, on their infant son, Andrew.

Andrew, born when his mother was fifteen and a half weeks pregnant, weighed just 1 pound, 12 ounces. He was never able to breathe on his own. Even with a respirator's help, Andrew's lungs frequently stopped working and he suffered bouts of pneumonia. He was plagued with infections, abscesses, and gangrene. Unable to take nourishment, he lost weight. His brain stopped growing at three weeks. Lack of vitamins and minerals led to rickets and broken bones. "The only time I have seen x-rays of more fractured bones was in an air force crash victim," was one doctor's comment. "It hurts like hell every time he takes a breath," said another.

Nevertheless, the doctors kept Andrew breathing for six months. Repeatedly, his mother and father begged them to turn off the respirator. The doctors refused. The Baby Doe Rule was not in effect then, of course, but Andrew's doctors threatened to take the Stinsons to court if they did not continue to permit treatment.

Clearly, Andrew's case was very different from Baby Doe's. The latter needed only a simple operation to live; the former would have survived only the briefest time without massive human assistance. The two infants represent extremes. Most babies who would be affected by a Baby Doe Rule would not. They would fall somewhere between the two—more severely handicapped than Baby Doe but not so hopelessly ill as Andrew Stinson. How do we decide whether or not to treat those in-between babies? Where do we draw the line?

According to some people, including members of Right-to-Life, a line cannot be drawn. Once doctors permit one handicapped baby to die, they open the door to allowing them all to die. Here is another slippery slope, Right-to-Lifers warn. Failure to do everything possible to save an Andrew Stinson would lead directly to the deaths of thousands of helpless unwanted babies.

Others reject the slippery slope argument. Drawing the line may be difficult, they say, but it can be done. Doing it requires designing a Baby Doe Rule flexible enough to allow each case to be decided individually. Then doctors and parents will be able to give treatment when it is appropriate and to withhold it when it is not.

A second major concern among those commenting on the revised Baby Doe Rule had to do with the quality of life. To what extent should that quality be considered when it is a question of whether or not to try to save a handicapped infant's life?

Quality of Life: Does It Count?

Again, Baby Doe and Andrew Stinson provide an illuminating contrast. A single physical abnormality corrected, the former might have lived thirty or forty years, perhaps longer. His retardation might have been only moderate. He could have known joy, warmth, laughter. He might have had friends, a simple job, a partly independent life of his own.

Not so Andrew Stinson. Not only had his brain stopped growing and developing, but as time passed, he underwent a series of brain seizures. Had he lived, he would have been profoundly retarded. His awareness of the world and of other people would have been virtually nonexistent. He would have been physically handicapped too, and perhaps in great pain.

To some such differences in life prospects are irrelevant. The Association of Retarded Citizens (ARC) is adamant on this point. In deciding whether to attempt to save an infant's life, says one ARC spokesperson, ". . . no quality-of-life or other such considerations are acceptable."

Others share this view. In October 1983, another Baby Doe—this one a Jane Doe—was born in New York state. The baby had several severe mental and physical handicaps.

Baby Jane's doctors offered her parents two alternative courses of treatment. With major surgery, they could correct some of the baby's worst physical problems. That might allow her to live as long as twenty years, blind, profoundly retarded, paralyzed, and in constant pain. Or the doctors could refrain from major surgery and simply correct some of the baby's lesser problems. Doing so would relieve much of her physical suffering but would markedly reduce her lifespan. After consulting with the doctors, social workers, and their priest, Baby Jane's parents chose the second alternative.

And quickly found themselves in court. A New York lawyer named Lawrence Washburn heard about Baby Jane through a Right-to-Life hot line. He brought suit to remove the infant from her parents' custody and to appoint a legal guardian who would obtain a court order forcing her doctors to perform the more drastic life-prolonging surgery.

Washburn's action found strong support among Right-to-Lifers and within President Reagan's administration. Lawyers for the federal government's Justice Department entered the case, suing the hospital to obtain Baby Jane's confidential medical records. The United States Surgeon General stated his opinion that the Does had violated their daughter's constitutional rights by refusing major surgery. "If we [federal officials] do not intrude into the life of a child such as this, whose civil rights may be abrogated," he told news reporters, "the next person may be you."

The court was not convinced by this slippery slope argument. In November, a federal judge backed the Does' right to deny treatment, saying that their decision had been based on "a genuine concern for the best interest of the child." The judge also blocked the Justice Department's effort to obtain Baby Jane's files.

The Baby Jane Doe case helped dramatize the battle between those who differ over whether or not quality-of-life considerations should be taken into account in assessing treatment possibilities. It also demonstrated the difference of opinion between people who believe families should be allowed to select medical care for those unable to choose their own course of treatment and those who say government and the courts must determine what care shall be given.

Should Families Decide?
Some people fear that allowing families to select treatment for the mentally incompetent will lead to an upsurge in deaths of infants, the elderly, the retarded, and others whose relatives or guardians consider them mentally or physically deficient. "The last person I want to decide whether I should live or die is someone for whom I'd be a burden," says Dr. Norman Fost, a bioethicist at the University of Wisconsin. "I would rather have the cleaning lady decide."

Peggy and Robert Stinson do not share Dr. Fost's point of view. They wanted Andrew's respirator turned off, not because he was a burden to them, but because they believed that continued life was an intolerable burden for *him*. "Until our legal and moral codes become sophisticated enough to cope with our machinery," the Stinsons wrote, "parents must have the right to decide whether or in what circumstances their tiny babies should be attached to respirators."

By late fall 1984, the law did seem to be catching up. On October 9, President Reagan signed into law the Child Abuse Prevention and Treatment Act. An amendment to that law tackled the Baby Doe issue head-on.

The amendment was the result of a long process of compromise. Six United States senators, including one who is a strong advocate of the Right-to-Life position, spent weeks debating its wording. As finally passed by Congress and signed by the President, the new law defines child abuse in a way that includes "withholding of medically indicated treatment from disabled infants with life-threatening conditions." That means that anyone who does withhold treatment has committed child abuse and may be punished through the courts.

However, the law goes on to state that treatment need not be given if it would be "virtually futile" in saving a child's life. Nor need it be given unless it would succeed in "ameliorating or correcting all of the infant's life-threatening conditions."

Most concerned groups—Right-to-Life, organizations that represent the handicapped, associations of health professionals—approved of the new law. The American Academy of Pediatrics, which had opposed the original Baby Doe Rule, hailed the new compromise as a "significant victory."

In June 1985 the U.S. Supreme Court agreed to consider the legal rights of severely handicapped infants and those of their parents and doctors. The Court's decision was expected to answer this question: Does the federal law that protects handicapped children and adults against discrimination also require HCPs to employ every medical technique to prolong the life of even the most terribly disabled newborn?

American courts continue to be involved in other medical decision-making as well.

Religion, Medicine, and the Courts

Pamela Hamilton, for instance, was neither an infant nor handicapped when she appeared in a Tennessee court in the fall of 1983. The twelve-year-old girl was perfectly capable of explaining to the judge why she and her family had rejected medical care for her.

Earlier that year, in June, Pamela's father had just taken her to the doctor with a broken bone. Immediately, the doctor noticed a large tumor on the girl's leg. The growth was the result of Ewing's sarcoma, a form of bone cancer. If Pamela were to live, the doctor said, treatment with anticancer drugs would have to begin at once. But Larry Hamilton refused to listen. The Hamiltons belong to the Church of God of the Union Assembly, a sect that accepts no medical care (except for the setting of broken bones). "Only God can heal," Hamilton told the doctor.

Like the doctors in Indiana's Baby Doe case, the doctors and hospital administrators in Pamela's case decided to seek a court order for medical care. Unlike the Indiana physicians, those in Tennessee got their order. After three months of chemotherapy, they reported that the growth on Pamela's leg had shrunk dramatically in size. A year later, however, the cancer spread to other parts of her body. She died at home in March 1985.

Was the temporary improvement in Pamela's condition justification for the court intervention? Would intervention have been justified if Pamela had lived? The Hamiltons' decision to refuse medical treatment was based on the teachings of their church. Under the Constitution, Americans have the right to live according to their religious convictions. Shouldn't they also have the right to die by them? Shouldn't Christian Scientists, who believe that healing comes through prayer, have the right to refuse to take drugs? Or Jehovah's Witnesses, who say it is wrong to accept blood transfusions, be permitted to decline them? Isn't forcing medical care on someone whose religion forbids it the same as forcing a devout Catholic to submit to an abortion?

In general, American courts have agreed that it is—provided the person refusing treatment is over the age of consent. An adult has the right to refuse medical treatment for a variety of reasons—religious beliefs included.

For children, though, it's different. Most courts have held that parents may not endanger their children's lives for the sake of their own religious convictions, however sincere they may be. The parents' freedom of religion does not extend that far.

In Pamela's case, though, some people worried about a possible violation of *her* freedom of religion. A twelve-year-old is capable of holding her own firm religious convictions. *Pamela* made it clear she believed that God alone could cure her. *Pamela* believed that it would be morally wrong for her to take anticancer drugs. No one who saw TV pictures of Pamela's frightened, tear-stained face as she was taken from her parents and rushed off in an ambulance could doubt that. On the other hand, are the religious convictions of a twelve-year-old necessarily the convictions she will hold all her life? The attorney who prosecuted the Hamilton case on behalf of the doctors thinks they may not be. "The girl ought to have the chance to become an adult to find out what her religious beliefs are," he argued.

Although Pamela probably would not have been forced to undergo therapy if she had been over the age of consent, there have been cases in which desperately ill adults have been ordered to receive medical care despite their religious feelings. Not long ago, a Maryland judge ordered a Jehovah's Witness to receive blood transfusions. His reasoning: the woman was the mother of five. If she died, her children would suffer. Therefore, the state had a responsibility to save her life.

To some that kind of reasoning seems dubious. It places the judge perilously close to the edge of another slippery slope. Where will the courts stop if they start ordering people to undergo medical care for the good of others? What might be the implications of such a trend in cases that involve abortions, fetal surgery, or people who need organ transplants?

Yet, what would the implications be if courts and the law did not make certain medical decisions with the public welfare in mind? Some of us may overlook how deeply involved government is in American health care. Concentrating on headline-making cases like those of Pamela Hamilton and the Baby Does, we forget that many routine medical matters are already closely regulated by the law.

Health, the Law, and You

For example, children must be immunized against several diseases—polio and diphtheria are two of them—before they go to school. In the case of outbreaks of some contagious diseases, such as hepatitis, quarantines must be observed. State laws may require public schools to check on students' dental health as well as on their sight and hearing and to recommend treatment if necessary. States have begun passing laws forcing parents to buy and use child safety seats in cars and trucks. There are laws to forbid the dispensing of unproven "quack cures" for serious illnesses. Other laws seek to protect our health by regulating the production, handling, and marketing of food and drugs. Health warnings must be posted on cigarette packages and advertising. In fact, we are surrounded by rules and regulations intended to protect our health and well-being and the health and well-being of our fellow citizens.

Are such rules justified? Some Americans think not. A few have gone to court to keep their children from getting vaccinations. Cancer patients have sued the federal government in an effort to obtain the drug laetrile, illegal in this country because it is considered ineffective, but which they are convinced will cure them. Many drivers resent being told that while driving they must strap their child passengers into protective seats. These people, like the Hamiltons and Baby Jane Doe's parents, regard some, at least, of this country's public health laws as intrusions upon their right to make private medical decisions for themselves and their families. "There is," says Laurence Thomas, assistant professor of philosophy at the University of North Carolina, "a limit to how much the state can *force* parents to do on behalf of their children."

Dr. Thomas might have added that there is a limit to how much the state can force people to do on their own behalf, as well. And he would have been right. The problem for the law, the courts, parents, HCPs, and the public is in deciding exactly where that limit is on the slippery slopes of bioethics.

9

A Right to Die?

The young man, barely out of his teens, had been injured in an auto accident. Rushed to a local hospital, he was placed on a respirator and connected to other life-support systems.

That was on a Thursday in early 1984. By the next Monday, although machines continued to pump the man's blood and move his lungs, his brain and body had lost all ability to function on their own. Doctors declared the man dead.

On Tuesday, they saw a muscle ripple in his foot.

How could it happen? Is it so difficult for a doctor to tell when someone has died?

It didn't use to be. Traditionally, doctors have defined death as "a total stoppage of the circulation of the blood, and a cessation of the animal and vital functions consequent theron, such as respiration, pulsation, etc." As recently as 1968, this was the definition of death in *Black's Law Dictionary*, considered an authority by legal and medical professionals alike.

But medicine has changed since the 1960s, and many of the old definitions must be discarded. Sophisticated equipment and new techniques now permit HCPs to resuscitate and save the lives of patients who would have had no chance of survival only a few years ago. Many of these people have almost literally "come back from the dead." Aware that a new definition of death was needed, the President's Commission for the Study of Ethical Problems in Medicine and Biomedical and Behavioral Research began to review the subject in 1978.

"Brain Death"

The commission submitted its report in 1981. It recommended that each state adopt a "definition of death" law, and that these laws be the same throughout the country. The commission's proposed statute reads in part: "An individual who has sustained . . . irreversible cessation of all functions of the entire brain, including the brain stem, is dead."

This amounts to a definition of death as brain death. Under it, a person who is maintained on artificial life-support systems may be declared dead when doctors can no longer detect any measurable brain-wave activity. In other words, people die when their brains die, despite what machines may be doing to maintain breathing or circulation. By 1984, thirty-seven states and the District of Columbia had passed brain-death legislation.

However, laws and definitions by themselves are not enough to solve thorny bioethical problems like those that surround the matter of death and dying. By the brain-death standard, the road accident victim *was* dead. Yet how could his doctors ignore that twitch?

What's more, bioethical questions are rarely limited to one clear-cut issue. Any individual case may be complicated by a variety of factors. The accident victim's doctors, for instance, had special cause for caution in determining his state. The man's family had agreed to allow his organs to be donated to people in need of transplants.

Who Lives? Who Dies?

One such person was waiting in a Memphis, Tennessee, hospital. He was Phillip Cockerham, a twenty-six-year-old carpenter with a failing liver. On Monday night, as soon as doctors had declared the accident victim dead, physicians in Memphis began preparing Cockerham to receive a transplant.

Then the "dead" man moved. Both operations were hastily cancelled. Cockerham left his hospital bed and went home.

Gone, at least for the time being, was his chance for a life-saving transplant.

Was the doctors' decision to cancel right? That decision seemed likely to cost Cockerham his life. Nor did it seem probable that it would do much to benefit the accident victim. Even after doctors saw his muscle move, they still considered him clinically dead. In any case, they knew that the damage to his brain— he had suffered head injuries—was so severe that he would never think, or feel, or sense anything ever again. By contrast, Cockerham had every reason to hope that given a healthy liver, he would live a full, normal life.

Tough as the decision not to operate may have been ethically, in practical terms it was the only decision possible. If the public ever came to suspect that doctors might hurry to declare people dead in their eagerness to obtain needed organs, it would surely mean an abrupt end to donations.

Ironically, of course, the accident victim's life—if he *was* alive on Tuesday—was actually extended by his having been intended as a donor. Had he not been, he would not have remained on life-support systems hours after his "death." Besides, it may have been largely because he was scheduled to become a donor that doctors were so sensitive to the possibility that he was still living. Such a tiny sign of life as that twitch might have been overlooked had the physicians not been so aware of their ethical responsibility regarding the use of cadavers as sources of transplantable organs. Without that awareness, the man might have been given up for dead days earlier. That is because in hospitals around this country HCPs do sometimes take people who are still technically alive off life-support machinery under certain circumstances.

At first, this seems a direct violation of the Hippocratic oath and of other codes of medical ethics. HCPs are enjoined by their oaths to preserve life. Over the ages, resisting death has been regarded as medicine's ultimate goal.

But HCPs point out that their professional oaths also require them to relieve suffering. In modern American hospitals, they stress, the two promises are frequently at odds with each other. To preserve life, it may be necessary to impose terrible suffering. To relieve that suffering may require doing something that ends a life. The conflict presents HCPs with an agonizing bioethical dilemma: When, if ever, does a patient have the right to die?

Karen Quinlan and the "Right to Die"

One of the first cases to bring this dilemma before the public involved a young New Jersey woman named Karen Quinlan. In 1975, Karen, then age twenty-one, slipped into a deep coma. At a hospital near her home, Karen was attached to a respirator. Then began a time of waiting.

Waiting—for what? Karen's doctors warned the Quinlans that their daughter was never going to wake up from her comatose state. Her brain was too badly damaged for that to happen. But neither would she necessarily die, doctors added. Kept on life-support systems, Karen might live for many years. An Illinois woman, thrown from a horse in 1956, survived in a coma for eighteen years before dying.

Eighteen years! The prospect seemed unbearable to the Quinlans. After days of anguished prayer and discussion, they asked the doctors to turn the machinery off and allow Karen to die. The doctors refused, and the case went to court.

There, the Quinlans presented their view: Karen had a right to die. In this, they had the backing of their parish priest and of the Roman Catholic Church itself. Death is a natural process, Catholic theologians argue, one rightfully governed by God alone. Although human beings may seek to save lives through surgery, medicine, and so on, they are not required to use "extraordinary" means—like those being used on Karen—to prolong life to the last possible moment.

The judge in the Quinlan case disagreed and ruled against Karen's parents. They appealed the decision, and finally, on March 31, 1976, they won the right to have their daughter's respirator turned off.

Contrary to most people's expectations, however, Karen proved to be able to breathe on her own. Eventually, she was moved from the hospital to a nursing home. She died there, still off the respirator, in June 1985.

In most cases, though, "pulling the plug"—turning off a respirator or other life-support systems—does result in death. Is that death a merciful release? Or a form of murder? In part, the answer depends on where you are.

Pulling the Plug on the Terminally Ill

In 1981, two California doctors were charged with murder after they removed life-support systems from a comatose man. The doctors acted at the request of the man's wife, who contended that her husband would not have wanted to survive in a vegetablelike state. (Later, however, the wife said that the doctors had not fully discussed the case with her before they pulled the plug. She filed a malpractice suit against them.)

First, the doctors turned off the comatose man's respirator. Two days later, they removed the IV tubes through which he was being fed. Not long afterward, the man died.

The district attorney who brought the murder charge against the doctors apparently did so at the request of Right-to-Life groups. His charges were quickly thrown out by a California appeals court. The judges ruled that the doctors' action had been justified by the medical facts in the case. Physicians, they said, have no obligation to continue treatment "once it has proved to be ineffective." Furthermore, removal of life-support machinery "is not an affirmative act but rather a withdrawal or omission of further treatment." In other words, the doctors did not *do* anything that caused their patient to die. He died because of what they did *not* do.

Not everyone accepts the distinction. In a New Jersey case, a court came up with a ruling that runs counter to the one in California. Here, the patient was an eighty-three-year-old woman. She was not comatose, but she was considered mentally incompetent, since she could not communicate and appeared to have little awareness of what was going on around her.

In 1982, the woman's foot and leg became severely ulcerated, the result of diabetes. Doctors asked her legal guardian for permission to amputate, but the guardian refused to give it. At the same time, the guardian asked the doctors to remove the tube through which the patient was being fed.

Although a lower court granted the guardian's request, the appeals court later denied it. (In the meantime, the patient had died, feeding tube still in place.) Unlike the California court, the one in New Jersey decided that disconnecting a feeding tube is a positive action. With the tube in place, the woman might have died of blood poisoning, or heart failure, or any one of a number of already-existing ailments. Removing it would have subjected her to an entirely new condition—starvation. "Thus," the court concluded, "she would have been actively killed by independent means."

What all this adds up to is that while the California court saw no difference between removing a feeding tube and turning off a respirator, the New Jersey court did. To the New Jersey judges, denial of nourishment would have been murder.

The AMA echoes the New Jersey court's stand. According to official AMA policy, it can be ethical for a doctor to cause a patient's death by stopping treatment in some cases. Taking a positive action that will hasten death, on the other hand, is "contrary to the most fundamental measures of human worth and value."

But what is the measure of human worth and value? To the parents of a girl named Andrea, whose case is cited in a Hastings Center publication, it seems to involve more than a simple choice between life and death.

Andrea was nine when she died of complications arising from cystic fibrosis. In the previous twelve months, she had been hospitalized eight times. Besides having breathing problems, Andrea was poorly nourished and weak. She showed no interest in anything and would speak only to her mother. Andrea's parents, knowing how desperately ill she was, asked the doctors not to subject her to extraordinary life-prolonging measures. The doctors agreed.

But avoiding extraordinary measures was not enough, the parents decided as Andrea lay slowly dying. Obviously, the child was suffering horribly. Couldn't the doctors "do something," give Andrea a massive dose of some pain-killer that would speed up her death and end her agony? The doctors answered that they could but that they would not. State law, the AMA code, their professional oaths—all forbade it.

After forty-eight terrible hours, Andrea died. Her doctors had done nothing to hasten her death, but neither had they done all that they could have done to prolong her life. Had they acted according to "the most fundamental measures of human value and worth"?

Commenting on this case, James Rachels, professor of philosophy at the University of Alabama, calls the doctors' action "inconsistent." Clearly, by agreeing not to use life-prolonging equipment, they indicated that they thought it would be better for Andrea to die quickly. But if they thought that, Dr. Rachels asks, why would they refuse to shorten her life a little further? "If it was pointless for her to endure, say, a four-day period of dying, why should we choose a course that requires her to endure a two-day period of dying?" he demands. Dr. Rachels' conclusion: Giving Andrea a drug overdose "seems more consistent with the reasoning that motivates us not to prolong life in the first place."

The argument seems logical. If it is ethical to relieve suffering by omission (failing to use every means possible to prolong life), why isn't it equally ethical to relieve suffering through a positive action? Or turn the argument around. If it is ever wrong to permit a terminally ill person to die, isn't it always wrong? How can medicine and the law insist on a sharp distinction between passively allowing patients to die and actively helping them to do so?

Some say that the answer is that such a distinction is rooted in the past, in a time when medicine was simpler and HCPs did not have the elaborate life-sustaining technology they possess today. In those days, doctors could not bring people back from the dead. Death, when it came, was certain and final.

Not so today. Such is the effectiveness and potency of modern medical technology that it has already altered the very meaning of the word "death." Now it is forcing us to think anew about the meaning of "life," too, and about what gives life its value. At the same time, it is causing society to reevaluate some old ideas about the right to die and the ethics of euthanasia.

Euthanasia, Pro and Con

Euthanasia means good death. Another phrase for it is mercy killing.

Over the ages, many people facing slow and painful deaths have sought euthanasia. Charlotte Perkins Gilman, the American feminist and social reformer, chose it when she was dying of cancer in 1935. In her last message, Gilman defended her decision. "When all usefulness is over," she typed, "when one is assured of an imminent and unavoidable death, it is the simplest of human rights to choose a quick and easy death in place of a slow and horrible one. . . . I have preferred chloroform to cancer."

But to many people, what Gilman and others like her have done is not "chosen a quick and easy death," but "committed suicide." When a patient who decides on euthanasia succeeds in getting the cooperation of an HCP, a murderous action compounds the suicidal one.

The Catholic Church is outspoken in its opposition to euthanasia. In 1980, Pope John Paul II issued a declaration in which he rejected mercy killing as objectively and universally wrong. Like the AMA, however, Catholic theologians distinguish between "active" and "passive" euthanasia. The Church does condone the disconnecting of life-support systems in certain situations, such as the one faced by Karen Quinlan.

Catholics and others who oppose euthanasia have a number of specific reasons for the position they take. Many regard euthanasia as yet another slippery slope. First doctors take the comatose patients off respirators. Then they refuse to feed them. After that they try to starve those who aren't even in comas—just unable to talk or feed themselves. Who will be next? The blind? The middle-aged?

And what about HCPs who may be corruptible? One might agree to end the life of a patient whose continued stay in the hospital is a financial burden to his family. Another might accept a bribe to do the same to someone's rich aunt or grandmother.

The idea that hundreds of people may come to rely on euthanasia as a legal way to do away with unwanted relatives seems a real threat to many.

Another threat is that euthanasia could be turned into something with no resemblance at all to killing out of mercy or pity. Forced euthanasia might be used to eliminate whole groups of people considered to be undesirable. That is how Adolf Hitler used it during his twelve-year dictatorship in Nazi Germany. Jews, gypsies, Catholics, scholars, homosexuals—all were ordered into the death chambers. In this country, mass forced euthanasia might be a possibility for elderly people on welfare or for the retarded, those who oppose euthanasia warn.

Some people contend that permitting euthanasia would be a deathblow to modern medicine. "Legalized euthanasia would be a confession of despair in the medical profession," a Jesuit priest wrote nearly forty years ago. "It would be the denial of hope for further progress against presently incurable maladies." Since doctors and scientists would no longer be confronted with the suffering of the terminally ill, the argument goes, they would no longer feel impelled to develop cures or treatments for serious illnesses.

Currently, scientists do devote themselves to medical research, and that raises another argument against euthanasia. At any time, a new discovery could save the lives of hundreds of the terminally ill. "Cures can come down the pipeline at any hour of the day," says Dr. Marshall L. Bruner, of Fort Lauderdale, Florida. How would family members feel if they had okayed a mercy killing just days before a new drug became available?

Finally, there are those who argue that no human being has the right to decide that he or she—or anyone else—no longer has a life worth living, or that "all usefulness is over." That is what Charlotte Perkins Gilman thought about her life, but was she right? If nothing else, she could have offered herself as an experimental research subject, allowing anticancer drugs or painkillers to be tested on her body. That way her life would have continued to have a purpose, some say.

On the other side of the euthanasia debate are the people who argue that an individual's life belongs to that individual and to him or her alone. "What gives a physician the right to keep alive a patient who wants to die?" one man—burned, blinded, and crippled in a fire demanded bitterly. He had begged in vain to be permitted to die. A woman dying of a painful cancer has no obligation to suffer for months just to enable researchers to test a new drug, say those who favor making euthanasia legally available. A comatose man should not be forced to stay "alive" just to prove to society that he has not committed suicide. If a particular religion condemns euthanasia, that is fine—for members of that religion. But people of other faiths must not be compelled to abide by its moral dictates.

There is a puzzling inconsistency in the way our society regards mercy killing, say some who think euthanasia ought to be available to those who honestly want it. Society says euthanasia is wrong because it involves the taking of life. But society permits the taking of life in other ways. It sends people off to kill and be killed in wars. Over half the states allow criminal executions. Ethicist Joseph Fletcher sums this paradox up eloquently in his book *Morals and Medicine*:

> We are, by some strange habit of mind and heart, willing to impose death but unwilling to permit it; we will justify humanly contrived death when it violates the human integrity of its victims, but we condemn it when it is an intelligent voluntary decision.

What if the law were changed to allow euthanasia—or at least passive euthanasia—in certain circumstances? Could any precautions be taken to protect those who want to continue living?

Protecting the Terminally Ill

One precaution could be "living wills." A living will is signed by a person while he or she is in good health. It gives permission for that person's doctor to turn off life-support systems in the case of terminal illness or permanent coma. The purpose of a living will is to give those who have signed them some measure of control over their final days and weeks. At the same time, by *not* signing one, people can indicate their desire to be maintained on artificial support systems until every flicker of life is gone. In 1985, living wills were legal in twenty-two states and the District of Columbia.

Another obvious precaution would be to set up hospital euthanasia review boards, similar to the Institutional Review Boards that rule on human experimentation. Such boards would be required to approve any euthanasia request before it could be honored.

Euthanasia review panels would have to work closely with patients and with their families. They would have to help the terminally ill to clarify their own thoughts and desires, and to make sure that patients who request euthanasia are expressing their sincere wishes. They would have to guard against selfish family members who might have reasons of their own for encouraging a mercy killing, and be alert to overprotective families who, through love, urge euthanasia on a patient who is in pain, yet still wants to live. Finally, they would have to steer a cautious middle course between HCPs who do not want to admit that they have "failed" and that death is inevitable, and those who hope to obtain transplantable organs or to make a hospital bed available for a new patient.

Euthanasia and the Future

Back in 1935, when Charlotte Perkins Gilman chose chloroform over cancer, she predicted that euthanasia would soon be a common practice. "The time is approaching when we shall consider it abhorrent to our civilization to allow a human being to live in prolonged agony which we should mercifully end in any other creature," she wrote.

She was wrong. The idea of legalized euthanasia continues to horrify many people today. The moral objections to it are deep and strong, and the possibilities for abuse clear and terrifying.

Yet, in a way, Charlotte Perkins Gilman was right. As modern medicine has extended the barriers of life—and death—doctors have won a greater and greater measure of control over both. More and more, they and their machines have the power to determine the precise moment of death.

10

Ethics and Money

Esther T, an elderly New York City woman, suffered a heart attack during the midafternoon of an August Sunday. By six o'clock, she had been admitted to a neighborhood hospital.

There, Esther received the best of care, but it was to no avail. At about three o'clock Tuesday morning, she died. Her hospital stay had lasted a little over thirty hours. The total bill, including the doctor's $625 fee: $3,275.

This is not exceptionally high. In the United States, health care is very, very expensive.

Overall, in the early 1980s, Americans were spending $322 billion a year—nearly $1 billion a *day*—on medical care. That comes to about 10 percent of this country's gross national product, the sum total of all goods and services produced.

How do we pay such a whopping bill? Part is paid by each patient. Routine visits to the doctor's office, drug-store items, prescriptions—most Americans pay for them out of pocket.

But costs can add up fast in our high-tech medical world. The price of a hospital bed alone, without a doctor, tests, or medicines is well over $200 a day in most parts of the country. An appendectomy can cost about $4,000. The hospital bill for baby Andrew Stinson's six months of life was nearly $105,000. An organ transplant may cost as much as $200,000. To pay bills like these, millions of Americans carry private medical insurance.

Such insurance may be available through a person's place of work. At many companies, both employees and employers contribute to insurance costs. Under some business insurance plans, a worker's family may also be covered. Men and women who are self-employed must pay the entire cost of any medical insurance they hold.

Also helping to foot the country's medical bill are state and federal governments. In 1965, Congress created two programs aimed at making high-quality health care available to all Americans, regardless of age or income. These programs, Medicare and Medicaid, are paid for through public taxes.

Medicare and Medicaid: Programs and Problems

Medicare is run by the federal government. It provides basic hospital insurance and help in paying doctors' bills to people age sixty-five and over. Medicaid, operated through the individual states, does the same for the nation's neediest. In 1983, about 52.2 million Americans were on either Medicare or Medicaid. Each day that year, 800,000 Medicare-Medicaid patients saw a doctor; 300,000 were in hospitals, 90,000 in nursing homes. Altogether, in 1983, Medicare and Medicaid bills came to nearly $57 billion.

As far as improving health care for Americans goes, Medicare and Medicaid have worked well. The two programs have made doctors and hospitals available to thousands of men and women who would not otherwise be able to afford them.

Yet today, government health care programs, particularly Medicare, are being blamed for bringing about a crisis in American medicine. Medicare is the major reason, its critics say, why medical care has become so terribly expensive. At the same time, Medicare and generous programs offered by private insurors have helped intensify some of the bioethical dilemmas we have examined in this book.

How could a program intended to help people pay their medical bills cause those bills to skyrocket? Medicare "was a built-in invitation to spend more than necessary," answers Dr. Carolyne K. Davis, director of the Department of Health and Human Services' Health Care Financing Administration and a strong critic of past Medicare funding policies. As Dr. Davis sees it, Medicare administrators offered doctors and hospitals a blank check. In effect they said, "Give our patients the best care possible and send us the bill. We'll pay it, no matter how high."

The medical community took the administrators at their word. They put Medicare patients through elaborate—and expensive—diagnostic procedures. They ordered lengthy—and expensive—treatments; difficult—and expensive—operations; sophisticated—and expensive—drugs. Then they sent the government the bills.

The government paid the bills, and with those payments, physicians and hospitals invested in newer—and even more expensive—equipment; performed more daring—and even more expensive—operations; prescribed more effective—and even more expensive—medicines. Medicare bills climbed again, and Medicare payments followed suit. The companies that manufacture drugs, medical equipment, and surgical instruments, recognizing a growing demand for their products, spent millions on still more research and development. Even before the new products went on the market, doctors and hospitals were waiting to buy them.

Costs spiraled through the 1970s. Each new medical technique meant a bigger Medicare bill. Every bill was paid. And each payment meant improved technology. By 1980, Dr. Davis says, costs for hospitalized Medicare patients were rising at the rate of 19 percent a year. Over the next three years, the program's spending increased more than 60 percent. If the trend goes on, Dr. Davis cautions, Medicare will go bankrupt within the decade.

Medicare is not alone in facing overwhelming costs. Recent medical advances are naturally available to privately insured patients; and doctors and hospitals have presented private insurance companies with higher and higher medical bills too. That meant these companies had to raise their rates, and men and women covered by private insurance have seen the cost of their premiums soar. By 1984, a family of four headed by self-employed adults could be paying over $2,000 a year for just-adequate medical insurance. Officials at one major company, the Chrysler Corporation, complained that they were spending $6,000 a year in health insurance premiums for every one of their employees!

Bioethical problems were growing right along with costs. Why is the question of the right to die so much on people's minds today? Because hospitals now own all that life-prolonging machinery. Why the rethinking of the Supreme Court's 1973 abortion decision? Because new technology in the pediatric ward now means survival for incredibly tiny babies. Why is medical experimentation of growing concern? Because, thanks to public and private insurors paying for increasingly expensive drugs and operations, patients can withstand procedures that would have killed them just a few years ago. In fact, says one Washington, D.C., doctor, "You can't talk about ethics without talking about money."

The Business of Medicine

You never could. For ages, the popular imagination has linked money and medicine. As long ago as the fourth century B.C., the Greek philosopher Plato defended doctors against what must have been a criticism even then. "The true physician," Plato wrote in *The Republic*, " . . . is not a mere money-maker."

That is as valid a statement now as it was 2300 years ago. Ethical doctors always put patients before profits. Nonetheless, medicine is a business, and in the United States it is a very profitable one. In 1980, the median (middle-level) doctor's salary (after payment of professional expenses and before taxes) was $63,800. For surgeons, median taxable income was $83,300.

What's more, doctors represent only part of the medicine-as-business picture. Much of the medical profit goes elsewhere— to pharmaceutical companies, for example, and to businesses that manufacture equipment and supplies. In addition, there is a new profit-making element on the scene: the medical service chain. This is an element that is already bringing about profound changes in American medicine.

For-Profit Hospitals: the Advantages

One of the oldest medical service chains is a California-based company, American Medical International (AMI). In 1957, AMI consisted of just one medical laboratory.

From the first, the laboratory did a brisk business. California was a rapidly growing state in the 1950s, and there were plenty of Californians around to buy the lab's services. Soon, AMI was able to acquire several hospitals. With the 1960s, came the Medicare-Medicaid boom, and AMI took off. Today it is the nation's fourth-largest for-profit medical service chain.

How is an AMI hospital different from other American hospitals? Traditionally, hospitals have not sought to make a profit. Many hospitals have been public or community institutions. Others have been run by universities or religious organizations. Of course, every hospital—and every other medical facility—must have an income that equals or exceeds its costs in order to survive. The difference between a traditional institution and one run "for profit" lies in what becomes of that income.

In the traditional American hospital, any extra income is plowed right back into the institution. It is used to replace equipment, to build new buildings and renovate old ones, to meet the costs of staff salaries, and much more. At a company-owned for-profit hospital, too, a part of the profit goes for such purposes. But another part goes to the men and women who own the company. These people have invested money in the company and own stock in it. The for-profit medical chains are run along the same principles as any other profit-making enterprise. They are businesses, whose first responsibility is to satisfy their stockholders by giving them as much of a profit as possible.

By 1983, there were more than twenty-seven investor-owned hospital chains in the United States. Together, they own and operate about 1,000 hospitals. These hospitals produced gross revenues of $11 billion in 1983. That comes to about 10 percent of the American hospital business. Economic analysts believe that the chains' share will increase 25 percent each year between 1984 and 1989. Besides hospitals, medical service chains may own nursing homes, psychiatric hospitals, out-patient diagnostic centers, drug and alcohol rehabilitation clinics, laboratories, and speech and physical therapy centers.

By 1985, hospital supply companies were getting into the act, as well. In April of that year, the American Hospital Supply Corporation merged with the Hospital Corporation of America, the country's largest hospital management chain. Together, the businesses were worth $6.6 billion. Other similar mergers seemed sure to follow.

Those who invest in and run the chains are enthusiastic about their role in American medicine. They point with pride to the fact that in several places, the chains have saved failing hospitals. In Crawfordsville, Indiana, for instance, a sixty-year-old public hospital, Culver Memorial, was on the verge of closing its doors. The building was old and dilapidated. Plumbing problems were causing sewage to collect in the basement, and hospital administrators struggled in vain to meet fire-code regulations. Local officials wanted to raise taxes to provide money to improve the facility, but voters turned them down.

Then along came the AMI. It bought Culver and poured $17 million into rebuilding. People in Crawfordsville began looking forward to having a spanking new, modern hospital, courtesy of AMI investors.

Crawfordsville could also look forward to having a more efficiently run hospital than Culver used to be, AMI promises. Like other medical-service chains, AMI relies heavily on computers and automation to make things run smoothly. Furthermore, the company tries to target the specific needs of the people who are going to be its patients. If Crawfordsville turns out to need a special pediatric center, AMI may build one. If the need seems to center on care for the elderly, AMI will probably respond. If the greatest need is for diagnostic services for people living out of town, AMI may equip and run mobile diagnostic units in rural areas.

Not only are for-profit hospitals more efficient, their owners maintain, they are much pleasanter for patients to stay in. Rooms are carpeted and wall-papered. None of that yucky hospital green. Patients even praise the food at many chain hospitals. In Florida at Tampa Women's Hospital, which is owned by a chain called Humana, Inc., the parents of new babies feast on celebratory dinners of stuffed shrimp, filet mignon, and champagne.

Even as they are improving the amenities and increasing efficiency, for-profit owners claim, they are lowering patients' bills. By refusing to schedule any but emergency surgery on weekends, for instance, they reduce what they must pay in nurses' salaries. By concentrating on a community's greatest needs and streamlining their operations to meet those needs, they can cut each patient's share of the total bill. Such refinements as mobile units and out-patient emergency centers are reducing costs for some procedures by as much as 60 percent.

Will for-profit chains prove an unmixed blessing for American medicine? Critics do not think so. They dispute the owners' rosy picture on several counts.

For-Profit Hospitals: the Drawbacks

The chains' practice of taking over traditional hospitals is distorting the relationship between patients and the institutions that care for them, the critics say. In the past, hospitals existed, first and foremost, to offer health care. Today a growing number have the primary goal of making money. AMI did not buy Culver Memorial in order to improve the health of the people of Crawfordsville. Its aim was to produce a money return to investors. "A hospital's first obligation should be to the sick," says a professor emeritus at Harvard University Medical School. "They [for-profit hospitals] must think first of their stockholders."

The critics don't think that for-profit hospitals are necessarily more efficient than traditional hospitals, either. As evidence, they cite a report drawn up for the federal government's Bureau of Health Facilities. That report showed that investor-owned hospitals spend 30 percent more on overhead costs than traditional hospitals do.

Nor do the critics agree that patients' bills will be lower at most for-profit institutions. Some may be able to offer a saving, but the bureau's study indicated that overall, profit-oriented hospitals are 24 percent more expensive than others. An investigation by the General Accounting Office, an agency of Congress, revealed that costs may rise as much as $50 a day after a chain takeover. At Humana's Tampa Hospital, it costs $13,000 to have a baby. Across town, at Tampa's community hospital, it costs $3,000.

Why so expensive? One reason is that for-profit hospitals generally charge more for tests and medicines than other hospitals do. The average drug price markup at a traditional hospital is 20 percent. In a for-profit institution it is 80 percent. The huge margin is one way chains guarantee their profit.

The critics also express concern about the quality of the care patients will receive in profit-making hospitals. One chain, National Medical Enterprises (NME), hires as few licensed nurses and as many aides and unlicensed personnel as possible. NME recently cut its registered nurses from 40 percent of staff to 25 percent. That cost-cutting measure is sure to affect patients.

In another move to reduce expenses, Humana, Inc., decided not to open an already-constructed special center for the treatment of burns at its Louisville, Kentucky, facility. Not enough burn victims in Louisville to make it profitable, Humana executives decided. But while the center stood empty and unstaffed fifty-four-year-old Ila Davis, who lived just minutes away from it, died of burns after an explosion wrecked her home in 1983.

The most fundamental criticism of the medical-service chains, however, is that they are helping to create a two-tier system of medical care in the United States. On the top tier, receiving excellent care, are the well-to-do. On the bottom, and getting increasingly inadequate care, are the poor, the elderly, and the handicapped.

Such a two-tier system would not be unique to twentieth-century America. In most times and places, the rich have been healthier than the poor. But with the adoption of Medicare, Medicaid, and other government health-care programs, the United States seemed to have committed itself to moving away from such a system. Now, many fear, for-profit medicine is beginning to undo all that those programs have accomplished.

Those who feel this way point to buying and building patterns among the medical-service chains. Most of their facilities are in the "sunbelt" states of the South and Southwest. There, populations are growing and incomes are rising. In the North and East, where poverty is spreading, there are fewer investor-owned hospitals. What is more, nationwide the majority of for-profit institutions are in affluent suburbs rather than in poorer city neighborhoods. The hospitals' aim seems to be to serve those who can afford expensive medical care because of higher incomes and private insurance. Those insured through public programs must seek treatment in other types of hospitals. Too often, these hospitals, like the one in Crawfordsville, are decrepit and unable to offer the best care.

Some go so far as to accuse the for-profit hospitals of deliberately discriminating against the poor. A Kentucky woman signed legal papers alleging that a Humana hospital there would not allow her to take her newborn infant home until she paid an $8,000 bill. Another woman, this one in Tampa, tried to enter that city's Humana Hospital. "They just told me, they said, 'Either you give me cash, or we just transport you over to Tampa General,'" the woman told a reporter for the public television program *Frontline*. The woman—who did not happen to be carrying over $1,000 in cash—went to the community hospital.

The owners of the chain respond vigorously to the criticism. They deny that they discriminate against those in need or that they are helping to produce a double standard of health care. AMI points out that when it bought Culver Memorial, it agreed to establish a $3.8 million trust fund. Income from the fund will be used to provide low-cost medical care to the area's needy. Humana, reacting to public pressure, agreed to open its Louisville burn center after all. And for-profit owners reiterate their contention that over the long run taking a businesslike attitude toward medical care will allow them to increase efficiency as costs go down.

That may or may not happen. But meanwhile, others are taking immediate steps to reduce medical costs. Helping to lead the way is Medicare.

Prospective Payment: Cost-Cutter or Quality-Cutter?

Medicare's cost-cutting plan is called "prospective payment." Under it, doctors and hospitals will no longer receive a blank check from the federal government. Rather, they will have to predict ahead of time how much it will cost to treat each Medicare patient. Then they will receive that amount of money—no more.

The federal government is issuing strict guidelines for HCPs to use in making their predictions. The guidelines require each patient to be placed in a specific diagnosis-related group, a DRG.

Medicare has set standards for each DRG. A patient is classified according to age, sex, and illness. An eighty-year-old woman with heart disease will be in a different DRG from a sixty-five-year-old man with emphysema. A person with a severe heart condition will be classed differently from a person with a mild one. That is because the DRG guidelines also take into account the usual length of hospitalization for each condition and the normal course of treatment for it. In all, Medicare officials intend to recognize 467 distinct DRGs.

Once a patient has been placed in a DRG, the hospital will notify Medicare, and Medicare will pay exactly the amount it has agreed in advance to pay for anyone in that category. If costs for the patient's care go over that amount, the hospital must pay the difference. But if actual costs are less than Medicare has paid, the hospital keeps the difference. "We wanted . . . to give the institutions an incentive to change their behavior," says Dr. Carolyne Davis. "The best way to do that is to create a reward." Dr. Davis believes that prospective payment will force hospitals to keep bills down. Many in the health care field say she is correct.

Medicare began using its new payment system in the fall of 1983 and planned to have it fully in place by 1986. But even before Medicare adopted prospective payment, systems like it had gone into effect in four states: Massachusetts, New York, Maryland, and New Jersey. In those states, hospital costs are still rising, but the rate at which they are rising has slowed down.

Those who support cost-reduction plans like prospective payment believe they will stabilize more than Medicare bills. As private insurors see Medicare costs cut, they say, they will demand that hospitals keep costs under control for them as well. Already, a number of private insurance companies, such as Blue Cross and Blue Shield, are taking steps to be sure that hospitals charge as little as possible per patient. In Kansas, Blue Cross/Blue Shield put its own statewide prospective payment plan into effect in January 1984.

Proponents of prospective payment expect that it will eventually reduce doctors' bills, as well as those from hospitals. As hospital administrators attempt to lower their costs, they will urge physicians to begin ordering less expensive tests, drugs, and treatments for their patients. That will mean another saving, one that will eventually affect private insurors and patients.

Whether prospective payment accomplishes all that Dr. Davis and others hope remains to be seen. But most people, no matter how optimistic, believe that even if it does, Medicare will continue to be a health-care system in trouble. In the early 1980s, the Congressional Budget office estimated that if prospective payment saved Medicare $100 billion by 1995, the system would still be $300 billion in debt. Why? Because the United States' elderly population is growing so rapidly. In the mid-1980s, about five people were paying into Medicare for every person who was receiving benefits from it. But as more and more Americans reach retirement age, that ratio will change. By the year 2050, Dr. Davis projects, there will be only 2.6 contributors for every beneficiary. Unless Congress changes the way Medicare is funded, its income will drop while its costs continue to rise. Prospective payment will not alter that fact.

In other ways, too, prospective payment may prove to have drawbacks, drawbacks that are not apparent to everyone right now. Dr. Davis, for instance, foresees an era of increased medical efficiency as each hospital begins to specialize in just a few procedures instead of trying to treat the widest possible variety of illnesses and conditions. Like fast-food outfits that cut costs by limiting their menus, specialty hospitals could deliver care more quickly and cheaply than today's full-range institutions.

That is fine in a big city, where McDonald, Burger King, Kentucky Fried Chicken, and the Pizza Hut are all on the same block. But what about the country, where eating places are few and far between? People don't want to be stuck with nothing but hamburgers. The same is true of hospital care. People in sparsely populated areas need full-range hospitals. They can't live with just a few specialty institutions. But will full-range hospitals be able to cut costs and survive?

Some people worry about the survival of quality medical care all-round. Dr. Frank Primich, president of the medical staff at Riverside General Hospital in Seacaucus, New Jersey, is one of them. Already, the quality of care is slipping in his state, Dr. Primich charges. New Jersey instituted a prospective-payment plan in 1980. The Medicare plan is modeled on it.

"There is a cutting in the quality of care," says Dr. Primich. Such a cutting is inevitable with prospective payment, he contends. "If you put a lid on costs and lower them . . . something has to give. What gives is the expenditures designed to deliver quality care."

Dr. Primich made this charge on the *MacNeil/Lehrer News-Hour*, a program carried nightly over television's Public Broadcasting System. When co-host Jim Lehrer asked for specific examples, Dr. Primich did not hesitate. "One is that if an individual needs a certain medication that is expensive, [doctors] are beginning to find that it is not available in the hospital pharmacy. The pharmacy is stocking a preparation that is less expensive and, very frequently, less effective." By saving money on drugs, the hospital is increasing its chances of making a profit, even under prospective payment.

The doctor mentioned other problems. One of the most serious, he claimed, is that patients are being sent home from the hospital too soon, before they are well enough to go. "Once you establish that the hospital is going to be paid the same amount, the sooner the patient is discharged, the greater 'the profit' or the less the loss . . . so that there are pressures [on doctors] to discharge patients . . . early."

But are doctors obliged to respond to that pressure against their best medical judgment? Yes, answered Dr. Primich. "For our own self-preservation, we must make those cuts that they [hospital administrators] suggest. Otherwise, the hospital will become insolvent, and I will not have a place to practice."

The problems that concern Dr. Primich could affect all hospital patients. Yet it seems certain that they will be worse for people who are on Medicare or Medicaid. The elderly, the handicapped, the needy will always be more vulnerable and easier to disregard, than those who are young, strong, and working at good jobs. In a medical world in which individuals and institutions must be as concerned about profits as about patients, it will be the affluent who will be best equipped to protect themselves and their interests. The rest will have to take what they can get.

Is that what America is headed for—a health-care system in which power and money determine who gets the best care?

11

Thinking About Bioethics

The study of bioethics is filled with paradoxes. It may be unethical to carry out certain experiments on human beings, yet without those experiments, medical progress could grind to a halt. It seems wrong to hasten the death of a suffering child—and just as wrong not to. HCPs abort two-pound fetuses in one part of a hospital, then go to another floor and fight to save the lives of even smaller infants. Over $100,000 goes to prolong the life of a hopelessly-ill infant, while a woman dies from burns it wasn't profitable to treat. Doctors debate the ethics of altering human genes, yet have trouble explaining to patients exactly what is wrong with them. Practitioners of the healing art attend executions and mete out medical punishments. Patients' rights may be more of a theoretical possibility than a practical reality. Government programs aimed at improving the health care of millions end up sending medicine into a financial crisis. Treatment that seems quite ethical at one time appears unacceptable at another.

Can the paradoxes be resolved? Bioethicists are trying.

Bioethics is a new concept, one that owes much of its being to the sophistication of late twentieth-century medicine. Yet this is not the first time medicine has faced the challenges of new technology.

Nearly 150 years ago, doctors in Europe and America learned of one of the greatest medical advances of all time: the use of an effective anesthetic. It was in 1846 that anesthesia was first used in a surgical procedure at Massachusetts General Hospital in Boston. Before then, doctors had had to choose between inflicting agony by operating on conscious patients or watching those patients die of such ordinary conditions as appendicitis, kidney stones, and massive infections.

But the introduction of anesthesia was not without controversy. Some doctors strenuously opposed its use. They were joined by a number of clergymen and other moralists.

Why the opposition to this tool of medical mercy? God has placed mankind here on earth to work and suffer. Any human invention intended to relieve that suffering must be the work of the devil. Nineteenth-century moralists were particularly outraged by the use of ether to help women in childbirth. After all, what had God told Eve? "In sorrow thou shalt bring forth children." Clearly, God *wanted* childbirth to be painful.

It did not take long to overcome such objections to the use of anesthesia. Doctors and laypeople alike learned to change their ways of thinking about the moral issues involved. Soon, anesthesia was making possible operations that surgeons had never considered attempting before. It had become an accepted means of easing suffering and of saving thousands of lives.

Like the men and women of the mid-nineteenth century, we face great changes in medical technology. Like them, we must look at the changes honestly and ask ourselves whether we need to adapt some of our thinking to encompass them.

We might change our thinking about death, for example. Since the beginning of human history, people have regarded death as the last great enemy. The ultimate medical aim has been to thwart it, to preserve life.

But is death still the final foe? Countless people, experiencing the death-resisting mechanisms of a modern American hospital see it instead as peace and a release from suffering. So do their families. "When she finally died, I knew there was a God," wrote one Florida woman after spending months watching her sister die of cancer. For these two, death arrived as a welcome friend. To them, the ultimate enemy had been life—life sustained by hospital machinery, life that consisted merely of the maintenance of basic bodily functions, with all personality, all spirituality, forever gone.

Does God demand the prolonging of soulless life? Some think so, just as, 150 years ago, some thought women must suffer terribly in bearing children. But ideas changed then, and they may change now.

Changing ideas about death could mean that people with fatal illnesses will be permitted to die a few months earlier and a great deal more comfortably than they are today. It could mean an enormous reduction in the suffering of thousands of patients, young and old.

A change in attitudes about death could have other effects. If they are not to be subjected to the ultimate in life-prolonging technology, patients might be able to stay at home and die there, surrounded by their loved ones. Those for whom death at home is not possible might spend their last weeks in a hospice instead of a hospital. Unlike a hospital, a hospice is committed to managing pain rather than to treating largely untreatable symptoms. Hospice patients are helped to die as comfortably and peacefully as possible. Today, there are about 1,300 hospices in the United States. Late in 1983, the federal government began offering some dying Medicare patients a chance to choose hospice rather than hospital care.

The new Medicare hospice program could benefit patients—and Medicare. Since hospices shun the life-sustaining drugs and equipment that hospitals invest in, their costs are lower. That could save money for the Medicare system, and for private insurors and patients as well. Thus one change—a change in the way we think about death and dying—could affect other bioethical issues.

There are other areas in which our thinking about medicine might change, and here, too, the changes could have far-reaching effects. The United States is a country committed to the idea that the most medical care is the best medical care. But is it?

In 1984, about 70,000 Americans were receiving kidney dialysis treatments. The cost of these treatments is enormous.

Are they all necessary? According to some estimates, up to half of those on kidney dialysis are seriously ill from other diseases in addition to their kidney problem. For them, dialysis is just one more element in the battle to stretch out their lives for another few weeks or months. Would it be morally indefensible to limit dialysis treatment to people who are otherwise reasonably healthy and who will therefore benefit from the treatment in the long run? If that were done, the savings would amount to millions of dollars a year. The money saved might be used to fund research into new ways to treat—and prevent—kidney failure.

Dying patients with kidney problems are not the only ones who may be receiving more medical care than they can truly benefit from. Many doctors routinely order $250 CAT scans for patients with simple tension headaches. CAT scans are great for revealing the presence of lesions deep within the brain, but they reveal nothing about tension headaches. At the Chrysler Corporation executives quote a study showing that of forty-one employees complaining of lower back pain who checked in at one hospital during 1981, nearly all were put through a series of expensive diagnostic procedures. The employees' average hospital stay was ten days; their average bill, over $3,000. Not one of the forty-one was operated upon. Every one of the costly tests proved negative.

Are patients and their doctors sometimes confusing elaborate, high-priced medical care with the medical care that is most appropriate for them? Many people are beginning to suspect that they may be. Rethinking old ideas about the most care also being the best care could save billions of dollars for patients, private insurors, and government health programs.

At the same time, it could help solve other bioethical dilemmas by making scarce medical resources available to those people who really need them. As it is today, an otherwise healthy person with kidney problems may not be able to receive dialysis because so many of the machines that exist are being used for the terminally ill.

Should medical care be rationed so that those who will benefit most can receive it? Should the dying be asked to step aside for those likely to live longer? Care for some be curtailed? The idea seems abhorrent to many in this country. But it is the way medical needs are met in some other nations, including England. "The British spend less than half as much per capita [per person] as we do on hospital care," wrote Henry J. Aaron and William B. Schwartz, M.D., authors of *The Painful Prescription: Rationing Hospital Care*. "The rate of coronary artery surgery is only 10 percent of that in the United States. Many British teaching hospitals lack even a single CAT scanner. The proportion of hospital beds devoted to intensive care in Britain is less than one-fifth that of America. The British perform about half as many x-ray examinations per capita as Americans do, and use only half as much film per examination."

Would the British way be good for the United States? Under it, some people would get less care than they do now. But others might get a good deal more. Even before the advent of prospective payment and for-profit medical chains, quality medical care was spread unevenly through the American population. According to John Conyers, Jr., a member of the House of Representatives from Michigan, cancers are increasing among black Americans at twice the rate they are increasing among whites. High blood pressure kills fifteen times more blacks than whites. Statistics from the Public Health Service show that life expectancy for whites is about seventy-five years. For blacks, it's under seventy. The death rate for black infants is twice that for white ones.

Would some system of rationing health care bring the two groups closer together? It bears thinking about.

Another American health care prejudice that needs consideration is the idea that medicine's sole aim is to cure. Curing is one aim, of course. But prevention is important, too.

More emphasis on prevention would affect several areas of bioethical concern. As Representative Conyers points out, many of the health problems of black Americans are related to the work place. Compared to whites, blacks are 20 percent more likely to die from diseases caused by working with or near hazardous materials. Blacks may live in more dangerous areas than whites, as well. In 1983, the General Accounting Office reported that 75 percent of this country's toxic-waste dumps were located in mostly black neighborhoods. Cleaning up the dump sites and making the workplace safer would go a long way toward doing away with two-tier health care in the United States.

Prevention might help us deal with other bioethical issues. Consider abortion. Of the 13,000 abortions carried out annually on women more than twenty-one weeks pregnant, by far the greatest number are performed on teenagers. The majority of these girls are ignorant about effective birth control and may not even know they are pregnant until they feel the fetus moving.

Prevention of abortion, including prevention of late abortions, could center on educational programs aimed at informing teenagers about birth control. Of course, many Americans feel that such educational programs are immoral in themselves. Unmarried girls and boys should not be encouraged to use birth control, they say. As we saw, the Department of Health and Human Services has attempted to discourage teen birth-control through its squeal rule. But which seems to be the greater moral problem, avoiding pregnancy in the first place, or birth control by abortion?

Thinking about prevention means thinking ahead and trying to work out ways to cope with theoretical bioethical issues before they become real-life concerns. People who are involved in bioethical debates need to try to think ahead in other ways, too.

The parents of Baby Jane Doe, the handicapped New York baby, report receiving hundreds of letters after Lawrence Washburn took them to court and made their tragedy public. Many of the letters, Mrs. Doe told a reporter for the CBS news program *60 Minutes*, came from the parents of other handicapped children. For the most part these parents strongly supported the Does' decision to reject major surgery for their little girl. They wrote, some sadly, some angrily, of their struggles to make life comfortable for their own children; struggles made more difficult by the fact that federal, state, and local governments are reluctant to help pay the tremendous costs of training, educating, and caring for the handicapped. The very officials who tried in court to force them to agree to surgery for Baby Jane, the Does point out, have resisted efforts to force government to do more to help the handicapped. While fighting on behalf of Right-to-Life groups, the Reagan administration has cut back drastically on funding for handicapped programs. It is fine for society to insist on saving the lives of infants like their daughter, the Does maintain, if society will follow through and help those babies later on. But having saved them, society cannot then wash its hands of their problems.

None of us can wash our hands of the problems raised by a child like Baby Jane Doe. Nor can we ignore the other bioethical issues that cry out for our attention in the 1980s.

The issues are complex and difficult. Resolving them will not be easy. We will find that many of the choices and decisions we must make will be painful ones.

And even when we have made them, that will not be the end. For the one sure thing about medicine is that it will go right on changing and developing. As it does, it will raise new bioethical issues, and those too we will one day have to face.

Bibliography

Chapters 1-11

Reich, Warren T., Editor in Chief, *Encyclopedia of Bioethics*, New York: MacMillan, 1982.

Chapter 2: The Rights of Patients

Barry, Vincent E., *Moral Aspects of Health Care*, Belmont, CA: Wadsworth Publishing Company, 1982.

Fletcher, Joseph, *Morals and Medicine*, Boston: Beacon Press, 1960.

Harron, Frank, John Burnside, M.D., and Tom Beauchamp, *Health and Human Values*, New Haven, CT: Yale University Press, 1983.

Hirshaut, Yashar, and J. David Bleich, "Choosing a Therapy When Doctors Disagree." *The Hastings Center Report*, Vol. 5, No. 2, April 1975.

Katz, Jay, "Why Doctors Don't Disclose Uncertainty." *The Hastings Center Report*, Vol. 14, No. 1, February 1984.

Taubenhaus, Marjorie, *The Rights of Patients*, New York: Public Affairs Pamphlet No. 535, Public Affairs Committee, Inc., 1976.

Chapter 3: Organs for Sale

Annas, George J., "Life, Liberty, and the Pursuit of Organ Sales." *The Hastings Center Report*, Vol. 14, No. 1, February 1984.

Arehart-Treichel, Joan, "The Organ Transplant Odyssey." *Science News*, Vol. 124, October 1, 1983.

Caplan, Arthur L., "Organ Transplants: The Costs of Success." *The Hastings Center Report*, Vol. 13, No. 6, December 1983.

Sun, Marjorie, "Organs for Sale." *Science*, Vol. 222, 1 Oct. 1983.

The Hastings Center: Ethics in the 80s, Hastings, NY: Institute of Society, Ethics and the Life Sciences, 1981.

Chapter 4: Medicine in the Courtroom

Anderson, Kurt, "A 'More Palatable' Way of Killing." *Time*, Vol. 120, No. 25, December 20, 1982.

Klerman, Gerald, and Gerald Dworkin, "Can Convicts Consent to Castration?" *The Hastings Center Report*, Vol. 5, No. 5, October 1975.

Serrill, Michael S., "Castration or Incarceration?" *Time*, Vol. 122, No. 25, December 12, 1983.

Chapter 5: Bioethics and Human Experimentation

Barry, Vincent E., *Moral Aspects of Health Care*, Belmont, CA: Wadsworth Publishing Company, 1982.

Colvin-Rhodes, Linda M., Michael Jellinek, and Ruth Macklin, "Studying Grief Without Consent." *The Hastings Center Report*, Vol. 8, No. 4, August 1978.

Eth, Spencer, Cheryl Eth, and Harold Edgar, "Can a Research Subject Be Too Eager to Consent?" *The Hastings Center Report*, Vol. 11, No. 4, August 1981.

Fox, Jeffrey L., "Guidelines for Artificial Heart Implants Revised." *Science*, Vol. 223, 27 January 1984.

National Academy of Sciences, *Experiments and Research with Humans: Values in Conflict*, Washington, D.C.: Academy Forum, 1975.

President's Commission for the Study of Ethical Problems in Medicine and Biomedical and Behavioral Research, *Implementing Human Research Regulations*, Washington, D.C.: U.S. Government Printing Office, 1983.

——, *Whistleblowing in Biomedical Research*, Washington, D.C.: U.S. Government Printing Office, 1983.

Randal, Judith, "Are Ethics Committees Alive and Well?" *The Hastings Center Report*, Vol. 13, No. 6, December 1983.

Sands, Mark, "The Barney Clark Story: Smooth Face Emerges From Some Bristly Squabbling." *Newsletter*, National Association of Science Writers, Vol. 31, No. 2, October 1983.

Shelp, Earl E., and Norman Fost, "Practicing Procedures on Dying Children." *The Hastings Center Report*, Vol. 10, No. 4, August 1980.

Sordillo, Peter P., and Kenneth F. Schaffner, "The Last Patient in a Drug Trial." *The Hastings Center Report*, Vol. 11, No. 6, December 1981.

Sun, Marjorie, "NIH Bill Passes House." *Science*, Vol. 222, 2 December 1983.

Chapter 6: At the Brink of Life

Abramowitz, Susan, "A Stalemate on Test-Tube Baby Research." *The Hastings Center Report*, Vol. 14, No. 1, February 1984.

Bleich, J. David, and Carol A. Tauer, "The Hospital's Duty and Rape Victims." *The Hastings Center Report*, Vol. 10, No. 2, April 1980.

Bok, Sissela, Bernard N. Nathanson, David C. Nathan, and LeRoy Walters, "The Unwanted Child: Caring for the Fetus Born Alive After an Abortion." *The Hastings Center Report*, Vol. 6, No. 5, October 1976.

Clark, Matt with Deborah Witherspoon," Surgery in the Womb." *Newsweek*, October 31, 1983.

"First Test-Tube Quads." *Parade Magazine*, February 26, 1984.

Fletcher, John C., "Healing Before Birth: An Ethical Dilemma." *Technology Review*, January 1984.

Fletcher, Joseph, *Morals and Medicine*, Boston: Beacon Press, 1960.

Trafford, Abigail, "Doctor's Dilemma." *U.S. News & World Report*, Vol. 93, No. 23, December 6, 1982.

Warren, Mary Anne, Daniel C. Maguire, and Carol Levine, "Can the Fetus Be an Organ Farm?" *The Hastings Center Report*, Vol. 8, No. 5, October 1978.

Chapter 7: Genetic Engineering

"Banking (on) DNA for disease diagnosis." *Science News*, Vol. 125, June 2, 1984.

Budiansky, Stephen, "NIH concedes part of Rifkin suit." *Nature*, Vol. 312, 8 November 1984.

Cave, Lynn J., "Linking Diseases to their Genes." *BioScience*, Vol. 34, No. 7, July/August 1984.

Gould, Stephen J., "On the Origin of Specious Critics." *Discover*, Vol. 6, No. 1, January 1985.

Grobstein, Clifford, and Michael Flower, "Gene Therapy: Proceed with Caution." *The Hastings Center Report*, Vol. 14, No. 2, April 1984.

Lacayo, Richard, "A Theory Goes on Trial." *Time*, Vol. 124, No. 13, September 24, 1984.

Lewis, Ricki, "Beating the genetic odds." *High Technology*, December 1984.

"Life: Patent Pending." *Nova* transcript #907, Boston: WGBH-TV, February 28, 1982.

Miller, Julie Ann, "The Clergy Ponder the New Genetics." *Science News*, Vol. 125, March 24, 1984.

President's Commission for the Study of Ethical Problems in Medicine and Biomedical and Behavioral Research, *Splicing Life*, Washington, D.C.: U. S. Government Printing Office, 1982.

Rifkin, Jeremy, *Algeny*, New York: The Viking Press, 1984.

Sun, Marjorie, "Rifkin Broadens Challenge in Biotech." *Science*, Vol. 225, 20 July 1984.

Weatherall, David, "On the track of genetic disease." *New Scientist*, 5 April 1984.

Chapter 8: Medical Care and the Courts

Brody, Baruch, and Jan van Eys, "Faith Healing for Childhood Leukemia." *The Hastings Center Report*, Vol. 11, No. 1, February 1981.

Crippen, David W., and Robert M. Veatch, "Laetrile: Cancer Cure or Quack Remedy?" *The Hastings Center Report*, Vol. 6, No. 6, December 1976.

Holden, Constance, "Government Intercedes in 'Baby Jane Doe.'" *Science*, Vol. 222, 25 November 1983.

———, "HHS Preparing to Issue New Baby Doe Rules." *Science*, Vol. 222, 23 September 1983.

——, "Revised 'Baby Doe' Rule Is Born." *Science*, Vol. 223, 21 January 1984.

Levine, Carol, Anthony Gallo, M.D., and Bonnie Steinbock, "The Case of Baby Jane Doe." *The Hastings Center Report*, Vol. 14, No. 1, February 1984.

Lyon, Jeff, *Playing God in the Nursery*, New York: Norton, 1985.

Paulson, Jerome A., and Laurence Thomas, "Should States Require Child Passenger Protection?" *The Hastings Center Report*, Vol. 11, No. 3, June 1981.

Plotkin, Robert, and H. Tristram Englehardt, Jr., "Mentally Retarded Hepatitis B Carriers in Public Schools," *The Hastings Center Report*, Vol. 9, No. 6, December 1979.

Stinson, Robert and Peggy, "On the Death of a Baby." *The Atlantic*, Vol. 244, No. 1, July 1979.

Wallis, Claudia, "The Stormy Legacy of Baby Doe." *Time*, Vol. 122, No. 13, September 26, 1983.

Chapter 9: A Right to Die?

Annas, George J., "Nonfeeding: Lawful Killing in CA, Homicide in NJ." *The Hastings Center Report*, Vol. 13, No. 6, December 1983.

Aroskar, Mila M., Josephine Flaherty, and James M. Smith, "The Nurse and Orders Not to Resuscitate." *The Hastings Center Report*, Vol. 7, No. 4, August 1977.

Daniels, Terry, "The Nurse's Tale." *New York Magazine*, April 30, 1979.

Fletcher, Joseph, *Morals and Medicine*, Boston: Beacon Press, 1960.

Leake, Hunter C. III, James Rachels, and Philippa Foot, "Active Euthanasia with Parental Consent." *The Hastings Center Report*, Vol. 9, No. 5, October 1979.

President's Commission for the Study of Ethical Problems in Medicine and Biomedical and Behavioral Research, *Defining Death*, Washington, D.C.: U.S. Government Printing Office, 1981.

Seligmann, Jean, "When Doctors Play God." *Newsweek*, August 31, 1981.

Trafford, Abigail, "Doctor's Dilemma." *U.S. News & World Report*, Vol. 93, No. 23, December 6, 1982.

White, Robert, and H. Tristram Englehardt, Jr., "A Demand to Die." *The Hastings Center Report*, Vol. 5, No. 3, June 1975.

Chapter 10: Ethics and Money

Anderson, Harry, "A Bid for New Prestige." *Newsweek*, October 31, 1983.

"Crisis at General Hospital." *Frontline* transcript #201, Boston: WGBH-TV, January 16, 1984.

Dentzer, Susan, "NME's Game Plan." *Newsweek*, October 31, 1983.

——, "The Big Business of Medicine." *Newsweek*, October 31, 1983.

"Medicare Payments." *The MacNeil/Lehrer NewsHour* transcript #2090, New York: WNET-TV, September 30, 1983.

Trafford, Abigail, "Doctor's Dilemma." *U.S. News & World Report*, Vol. 93, No. 23, December 6, 1982.

"Vital Statistics." *Time*, Vol. 122, No. 17, October 17, 1983.

Wallis, Claudia, "Putting Lids on Medicare Costs." *Time*, Vol. 122, No. 16, October 10, 1983.

Chapter 11: Thinking About Bioethics

Childress, James, and Joseph Fletcher, "Who Has First Claim on Health Care Resources?" *The Hastings Center Report*, Vol. 5, No. 4, August 1975.

Schiffer, R.B., and Benjamin Freedman, "The Last Bed in the ICU." *The Hastings Center Report*, Vol. 7, No. 6, December 1977.

Schulz, S. Charles, Daniel P. Van Kammen, and John C. Fletcher, "Dialysis for Schizophrenia: Consent & Costs." *The Hastings Center Report*, Vol. 9, No. 2, April 1979.

Index